THE
SHAPING
OF
MODERN
BRAZIL

THE SHAPING OF
MODERN BRAZIL

Edited by ERIC N. BAKLANOFF

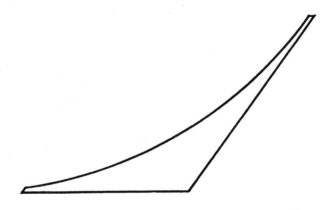

Published for the Latin American Studies Institute by
LOUISIANA STATE UNIVERSITY PRESS   BATON ROUGE

For Chris and Nicki

ACKNOWLEDGMENTS

THE PRESENT VOLUME EMBRACES SELECTED PAPERS DELIVERED AT THE Colloquium on the Modernization of Brazil held at Louisiana State University in Baton Rouge, February 23–25, 1967. The colloquium was sponsored by the Latin American Studies Institute and the Department of Sociology, with the generous support of the Wenner-Gren Foundation for Anthropological Research.

I am indebted to Professors Jane De Grummond, Wilfred Jokinen, Robert Flammang, Quentin Jenkins, and Robert C. West for serving on the Arrangements Committee and to Dr. L. A. Costa Pinto whose keynote address, "A Conceptual Framework for the Sociological Study of the Process of Transition," set the tone for the colloquium. Dr. Costa Pinto is Senior Research Officer at the United Nations Institute for Training and Research.

To Dr. Bernard Siegel, Professor of Anthropology at Stanford University, I am grateful for his careful reading of the entire manuscript and valuable suggestions, many of which have been incorporated in the text.

I am also grateful to Vanderbilt University's Graduate Center for Latin American Studies and to the Center for Advanced Study in the Behavioral Sciences, whose travel and research grants made my own paper included here possible.

vii

CONTENTS

INTRODUCTION

THE AIM OF THIS VOLUME IS TO EXAMINE A NUMBER OF CRITICAL variables and processes that have shaped contemporary Brazil: intellectual, social, political, economic, and geographic. Our view extends five centuries, from Brazil's colonial origin as a Portuguese colony to a prediction of the nation's landscape in the year 2000.

Each contributor is familiar with Brazil and has recently been engaged in research there. The choice of concepts, marshaling of evidence, and application of techniques reflects his particular academic field and the topic of concern.

With an estimated population of 90 million in 1969 and a land mass roughly equal to the United States without Alaska, Brazil is one of the large nations of the world. Still, as Professor Webb points out, Brazil's "effective territory" probably does not exceed one-third of the national territory. Brazil's population may reach some 225 million by the end of this century, assuming there is no check on its present rapid demographic growth rate. Though Brazil is large in numbers, her economic power translated into gross national product is no greater than that of the Netherlands and ranks substantially below the gross product of the 21 million persons comprising the United States Negro community.

The Brazilian landscape reveals an amazing coexistence of economic and cultural subsystems which bridge the time gap between prehistory and the present: the primitive hunting and food gathering groups immured in Amazonian *selva,* quasi-feudal estates in the remote hinterlands of Western Brazil, cottage industry in isolated towns, and modern industrial complexes in São Paulo State.

Brazil, writes Viana Moog, is "a cultural archipelago. And this archipelago is made up of many cultural islands, all more or less autonomous."

While not yet a major power among nations, Brazil has major power aspirations. And its influence in the Organization of American States and within what is loosely termed the Third World will surely increase during the last third of the twentieth century.

This book begins with Professor Cardozo's engaging paper on Brazil's colonial experience. With the Portuguese colony's official incorporation into the European trading area, Brazil was able, in the course of the sixteenth and seventeenth centuries, to monopolize the world production and export of sugar. Centered on Pernambuco and Bahia, the raising of sugar cane and its conversion into traditional sugar loaves "demanded a plantation-type industrialized agriculture." Coexisting with the coastal sugar economy was the raising of cattle in the interior by small farmers who took advantage of the Homestead Law (*Sesmarias*).

The incorporation of the West Indies into the world sugar economy, the advance of mercantilism in France and England, and the failure of the Brazilian planters to keep abreast of technical innovations conspired to end Brazil's preeminence as a sugar producer. Fortunately, the discovery and subsequent exploitation of gold in Minas Gerais "cushioned the depression that the decadence of the sugar industry had produced."

Cardozo also stresses the influence of cultural and intellectual currents in both metropolitan center and colony. Concerning Catholicism in Portugal (in the period following Trent) Cardozo wonders "whether or not a less rigid, less authoritarian, and less triumphal form of Christianity would not have produced better results on the level of human freedom and human welfare." He cites Adam Smith in his observation that by the middle of the eighteenth century "England had become one of the richest nations of Europe whereas Portugal had become one of the most beggarly." Clearly, the differential in economic position and intellectual climate between these two imperial centers would profoundly shape the subsequent development of their offspring nations in the Western Hemisphere.

With the close of the eighteenth century, the colonial system of monopolies and restrictions reached a *ponto morto,* a dead point, and the "liberal system" of John VI would now be called on to modernize Brazil.

The 1850's, in the words of C. H. Haring, "ushered in an era of unprecedented tranquility and economic growth" in Brazil. The period analyzed in my own chapter, "External Factors in the Economic Development of Brazil's Heartland: The Center-South, 1850–1930," was one during which the "liberal system" was given its full scope. Brazil's economy, particularly the Center-South region, was transformed and shaped by the international commodity, capital, and labor markets. The nation offered the natural resource base and unskilled labor; the rest of the world supplied much of the capital, technical know-how, and entrepreneurship.

Foreign capital played a decisive role in the construction, financing, and operation of railways, electric power plants, and urban infrastructure—and in forging the vital financial and commercial links between Brazil and the rest of the world. Foreign enterprise and its associated capital in Brazil represented the lateral extension of the emerging English and, later, American industrial revolutions. The human migratory current to Brazil accelerated in the 1880's and contributed notably to the Center-South's economic and social development. The partially assimilated immigrants introduced advanced technical and organizational methods and thereby raised the nation's capacity to absorb capital and deploy it more effectively.

In organization and structure Brazil, from mid-nineteenth century to 1930, typified what economists have come to call an "export economy." Coffee exports constituted the dynamic, autonomous variable which powered Brazil's economy; the foreign exchange proceeds from coffee also supported a rising volume of imports and increased the nation's capacity to service external debt and remit profits. Thus Brazil's highly specialized economy rested precariously on the world market for coffee.

With the disintegration of the international economy in the Great Depression, marked by collapse of coffee prices and the drying up of foreign capital flow, Brazil was compelled to seek a new development path: the "export economy" gave way to an "investment-government expenditure economy." The "Liberal System" gave way to "Dirigismo"—the active intervention of government in the economic life of Brazil under the guiding hand of Getúlio Vargas.

Professor John Dulles in his political biography, "The Contribution of Getúlio Vargas to the Modernization of Brazil," tells us that: "Behind a placid, friendly, benign exterior—the face of a man of infinite patience and good humor—lay a mind which was impatient, but which had been disciplined to wait." Vargas headed the Brazilian government (1930–1945) during the two most critical periods in the nation's political and economic life: the Great Depression and World War II. He used his considerable power and political skill to guide Brazil toward the ideal of an "autonomous industrial life" and to forge "one nation out of a collection of semifeudal states run by local party leaders with their own tariff walls, armies, and political machines."

In reaching the presidency again in 1951, Vargas took an active role in the creation of the National Economic Development Bank and the Bank of the Northeast, a major regional development institution. He demonstrated his pragmatic nationalism by establishing realistic conditions for the inflow of private risk capital from abroad and was instrumental in the organization of a joint venture involving a United States firm and the Brazilian government for the extraction of manganese in once-backward Amapá territory. This arrangement was to become an organizational model for subsequent mining enterprises in other Latin American countries.

Dulles leaves us with a portrait of a man whose public accomplishments and shortcomings contrast sharply with the "image" of Getúlio Vargas cultivated since his death by Communists and "ultranationalists" in Brazil.

Professor Busey's contribution, "The Old and New in the Politics of Modern Brazil," reminds us that in the long sweep of Brazilian political development, "nothing is more prevalent than this emphasis on paternalistic, elitist quasi-democracy." We should therefore not be surprised by parallel aspects of the governments of Emperor Dom Pedro II and current regimes. Both have exercised power with a combined reliance on authoritarianism in fact and democracy in form. The successful Brazilian chief of state exhibits identifiable characteristics: "He can be a strong political *fazendeiro,* though it is better that he also be an orderly and predictable one; but, in any event, he must be a good one. He must be merciful and generous with *o povo."* The *poder moderador* (moderating power) and use of extraconstitutional devices are cited as recurring features of Brazilian political life. Busey suggests that the "best" form of government for Brazil (constitutional democracy) may not be the feasible one at the present time.

Brazil's explosive industrial expansion after the Second World War has been a subject of considerable interest among economists. Did inflation stimulate or retard the development in Brazil? Why did the rate of industrial growth continue despite the sharp reversal in Brazil's terms of international trade after the fade-out of the coffee boom in 1954? Contradictory interpretations of sources and patterns of industrial growth abound in the literature. Dr. Donald Huddle's chapter, "The Postwar Brazilian Industrialization: Growth Patterns, Inflation, and Sources of Stagnation," examines several widely held interpretations of the nation's industrial growth for their compatibility with the available evidence. In applying systematic-empirical techniques, Huddle finds himself at odds on many points with Celso Furtado, Werner Baer, and the Economic Commission of Latin America. Among his findings: forced savings (induced by inflation) were negligible in capital formation; import substitution as a growth source was meager and at times negative, prior to 1953; labor migration to urban areas seems to have created a new dualism, for the industrial sector absorbed few of the migrants. In short, Huddle is skeptical of many of the benefits claimed for Brazil's postwar industrial drive, particularly in the light of alternatives foregone. Again, his explanation of the ultimate demise of industrial growth in 1962–63 is at variance with those of Furtado and Baer. For Huddle, a new emphasis on world markets together with reform in the primary sector constitutes the "necessary condition for increased long-run social welfare in Brazil."

Scholars have been giving increasing attention during the past decade to education as a modernizing agency. Investment in "human capital" is now considered to be a necessary concomitant of investment in tangible capital: plant, machinery and equipment, land improvements, etc. Dr. Saunders' chapter, "Education and Modernization in Brazil," provides us with an evaluation of the Brazilian system of primary, secondary, and higher education. Does the system create a population which is receptive to technical innovation? Does it diffuse among the population the organizational, administrative, and technical skills which support a modern society?

During the three centuries of Portuguese dominance, "education served to perpetuate a highly stratified colonial society." After independence the Empire evolved a dual educational system which, while providing minimal educational and artisanship skills for elements of the popular masses, continued to be "a system appropriate to a static society in which very little change occurred and none was contemplated."

The traditional system of education, however, became increasingly ill fitted to the requirements of a more prosperous and industrial Brazil. The aspirations of the rising middle groups, especially in the Center-South, created strong pressures after World War I for the expansion of academic secondary schools. These new secondary schools, mainly privately financed, served as a vehicle for intensified social vertical mobility. The very substantial increase in students completing their secondary education in turn created new pressures on institutions of higher education.

According to Saunders, the educational system in Brazil in the past quarter of a century has experienced tremendous growth: student enrollment in all levels—primary, secondary, and institutions of higher learning—has advanced at rates much greater than population growth. Consequently, the percentage of illiterates has fallen significantly among the young. His statistical analysis shows that the proportion of college students enrolled in "modern" subjects (in contrast to "traditional" law, medicine, and civil engineering courses) doubled in the period 1953–1964 from 16 to 32 percent.

While acknowledging substantial progress in quantitative terms,

Saunders notes the enormous qualitative gap which separates education at all levels in Brazil from parallel efforts in North America and Western Europe. Of higher education in Brazil he writes: "If the teaching function is vitiated, the research function is almost completely neglected."

In a remarkable concluding essay, Dr. Kempton Webb peers into the near (1980) and more distant (2000) future to determine the probable pattern of the Brazilian landscape. This landscape will be shaped by the interaction of millions of unconscious individual decisions, the natural resource base, and conscious decisions made by Brazilian planners on a large organizational level. Brazil's current landscape, Webb points out, is to an important degree the product of *devastaçao das matas,* the destruction of forest on sloping land. This process—"the gross sum of millions of individual acts" over a period of 400 years—has resulted in widespread erosion and brought havoc to the Brazilian land.

Webb reasons that the future configuration of Brazil's spatial development is intimately linked to the National Transportation Plan and its implementation. Since the 1950's, beginning especially with President Juscelino Kubitschek's Program of Goals, highways were extended and paved at a rate hitherto unequaled in Brazil's history. Brasilia, by its interior location, has become the destination for principal trunk highways. Highways and roads speed the physical integration of the Brazilian national territory and serve as "agents of economic and social change"; they become "ribbons of settlement" and foundations upon which subsequent development takes place. The official map which projects Brazil's highway pattern of the future reveals "a network or web which reaches out, amoeba-like, to touch and incorporate the remotest corners of the country . . . with tributary roads reaching out to establish contact with the borders of Guyana, Venezuela, Colombia, Peru, Bolivia, and Paraguay."

The success of Belo Horizonte and Brasilia, and the highway accomplishments to date suggest, in Webb's view, that Brazilians will henceforth put their imprint on their landscape with growing confidence and that by the year 2000 "Brazil will emerge to the eyes of the rest of the world as a massive, viable, productive, functioning state whose effective national territory will approximate the total national territory."

Between the present and the year 2000 Brazil's modernizing elites will be severely tested. Politically, they will have to evolve a framework that can reconcile progress and order with widening popular participation. Economically, they will need to ameliorate the condition of the poor (particularly in the Northeast) while maintaining the momentum of growth. Ideologically, they must harness the awesome energy of nationalism and direct it to constructive and functional ends. The continuing modernization of Brazil will rest, in part, on the making of a good bargain between the demands of nationalism and terms set in the international economy for the infusion of development capital, managerial expertise, and technology.

ERIC N. BAKLANOFF

THE
SHAPING
OF
MODERN
BRAZIL

The Modernization of Brazil, 1500-1808:

An Interpretative Essay

Manoel Cardozo

CAIO PRADO JÚNIOR, THE MARXIST HISTORIAN, SAYS THAT BY THE beginning of the nineteenth century Brazil had reached a dead point in its development. "The colonial regime," he wrote, "had achieved what it had to achieve. . . . The colonizing work of the Portuguese . . . had exhausted its possibilities," and there was nothing left to do.[1]

This was, after all, the view expressed by a number of people who were destined to live through the end of the Portuguese period. The Prince Regent himself, when he arrived in Rio de Janeiro on March 7, 1808 (having escaped the Napoleonic army that invaded Portugal), made it clear that he had come to found a New Lusitanian Empire,[2] and all his actions, before his abrupt return to Europe in 1821, were based upon the assumption that Brazil had to be modernized.

He began the process of change on January 28, 1808, immediately upon his arrival in Bahia on this side of the Atlantic. In Bahia, his stopover before sailing south to Rio, he signed the *Carta Régia,*

---

[1] *Formação do Brasil contemporâneo: Colônia* (São Paulo: Livraria Martins Editora, 1942) , 5-6.

[2] Luiz Gonçalves dos Santos, *Memorias para servir á historia do reino do Brazil, divididas em tres epocas da felicidade, honra, e gloria; escriptas na corte do Rio de Janeiro no anno de 1821 e offerecidas a S. Magestade Elrei nosso senhor o senhor D. João VI* (2 vols.; Lisboa: na Impressão Regia, 1825) , I, 5.

by means of which the ports of Brazil, heretofore closed to all but Portuguese shipping—in accordance with the prevailing theories of mercantilist economics—were opened to the shipping of every friendly country in the world. As José da Silva Lisboa, the pre-eminent Brazilian Liberal economist and contemporary of the Portuguese Prince John, gallantly wrote, the Regent's act may not have been more significant than the Magna Carta, which the English King John had been forced to sign,[3] but it marked the end, in more than a symbolic way, of the colonial system of monopolies and restrictions. Thanks to Prince John, Brazil was no longer to be a "garden, closed and forbidden to the rest of mankind . . . an unknown and forgotten country." No longer would foreigners, men of "diverse Nations," be kept from the satisfaction of living "under the shadow of the most Benign Prince on Earth," and contributing their knowledge of the new technology to the progress of Brazil.[4] No longer would Brazil be governed as in the past, when "its industry [was] repressed, its agriculture a matter of rote, its commerce little active and extensive, its population quite limited . . . ." [5] To the Prince Regent, as to Silva Lisboa, liberal economics would now be called upon to modernize Brazil.

Today, publicists like Caio Prado Júnior believe that liberalism has run its course, that it is no longer able to affect the modernization of Brazil. To them, liberal economics has reached in turn its dead point, and they naturally look forward to communism as the next age in the modernization of Brazil. I shall not make it my business to suggest what must be done to accelerate Brazil's on-going process of modernization, or even wonder whether or not modernization in itself is a good thing. My business is to look upon modernization in Brazil in historical perspective. I shall not be able to say much in the space at my disposal or document fully what I shall have to say, but I shall at least touch upon developments that characterized the period from 1500, when Brazil officially became Portuguese and therefore was incorporated into the European trading area, to

[3]José da Silva Lisboa, *Memoria dos beneficios politicos do governo de El-Rey Nosso Senhor D. João VI* (2nd ed.; Rio de Janeiro: Arquivo Nacional, 1940), 69.
[4]Santos, *Memorias*, 346–47.
[5]*Ibid.*, 344.

the arrival and subsequent administration of the Prince Regent, when the colonial system came to an end and Brazil took still another step forward in the process of modernization.

During the excitement of the spice trade, following the voyage of Vasco da Gama, the Portuguese paid little attention to their part of South America, which they early baptized the Land of the True Cross or of the Holy Cross. For almost thirty years they held their American colony for strategic reasons, largely to protect their route to the Cape of Good Hope and beyond to India and the Orient, but their hold was at best precarious. At the beginning, the Portuguese, as well as French interlopers, turned to the exploitation of one of the country's natural resources, the brazilwood tree, from which was extracted a reddish dye that was much in demand by the woolen manufacturers of Europe, and great quantities of logs were shipped across the Atlantic, as the records of the *Nau Bretoa* of 1511 candidly prove.[6]

The brazilwood trade must have indeed been considerable and rewarding, for, as Rocha Pita said: "It was that wood that gave its name to this opulent region, and contributed to its commerce and development (*grandeza*) since its discovery . . . ." [7] It was also galling, and shameful, to João de Barros, the Portuguese Livy and chronicler of empire, that so mean an article of trade should have overcome the cross upon which the Lord was crucified.

. . . since the Devil, through the sign of the Cross, lost the dominion that he had over us, by virtue of the passion of Christ Jesus that was consummated upon it: as soon as the red wood known as brazil began to be imported from that country, he labored to have this name used commonly by the people, and to remove from public memory the name of that wood that colored all the sacraments through which we were saved, through the blood of Christ Jesus that was shed upon it. And since I cannot in any other way avenge myself of the Devil, I warn all who this pas-

[6]See Bernardino José de Souza, *O Pau-brasil na história nacional Com um Capítulo de Arthur Neiva e Parecer de Oliveira Vianna,* Brasiliana, 162 (São Paulo: Companhia Editora Nacional, 1939) ; and *História da Colonização Portuguesa do Brasil* (3 vols.; Porto: Litografia Nacional, 1921–24) , II, 317–47.

[7]Sebastião da Rocha Pita, *Historia da America Portugueza desde o anno de mil e quinhentos do seu descobrimento até o de mil e setecentos e vinte e quatro* (2nd ed., Lisboa: Francisco Arthur da Silva, 1880) , 19.

sage may read, on behalf of the Cross of Christ Jesus, to give to this land
the name that with such solemnity was given to it, under pain that the
same Cross, shown to us on Judgment Day, will accuse them of being
more devoted to brazilwood than to it.[8]

Yet brazilwood was not the only attraction of the country that
refused to be called by its Christian name. The Portuguese found
monkeys and exotic plants and shipped them to Lisbon for the
homes and gardens of the landlubbers. They also found freedom
from the restrictions of European society. Even on Cabral's voyage
of discovery, the first time that the Portuguese, insofar as we know,
had set foot in Brazil, men from the expedition, before it sailed for
the Cape of Good Hope and the vaunted wealth of the East, fled
into the interior to join the natives, away from the light of their
civilization into the darkness of a Stone Age. Within a few years
other adventurers—Diogo Álvares, generally known as Caramuru,
in Bahia; João Ramalho, in São Paulo; and, southward, Cosme Fer-
nandes Pessoa, the so-called *Bacharel de Cananéia* (who really was a
mestre em artes from Coimbra) —found their way to Brazil. Some of
them were the victims of shipwrecks, beginning life anew among the
natives, constituting American families and raising the women that
would be given in marriage to the first bonafide settlers. How awesome life must have been among those who preferred the call of the
wild to the comforts of Europe, and how challenging. And how
sexually inviting to European males, whose appetites for the flesh
were always held in check by the majesty of the law and the moral
might of the Catholic church. In 1528, according to Rodrigo de
Acuña, more than three hundred Christians and children of Christians lived in Pernambuco amid temptations of such devastating
order that a Christian stood a better chance of salvation in the
depths of heathen Turkey.[9]

Alexander Marchant has touched upon these earlier days, when
business was conducted on the basis of barter,[10] as was the dyewood

[8]João de Barros, *Asia de Joam de Barros dos feitos que os portugueses fizeram no
descobrimento e conquista dos mares e terras do oriente,* ed. António Baião (4th ed.;
Coimbra: Imprensa da Universidade, 1932) , V, 174–75.

[9]*História da Colonização Portuguesa do Brasil,* III, 89.

[10]Alexander Marchant, *From Barter to Slavery, The Economic Relations of Portu-*

trade, but this was hardly the kind of economy that one could depend on. In time, the Portuguese had perforce to turn to something more dynamic, and in time they turned to plantation agriculture, making Brazil, in the words of Celso Furtado, "the first region in the western hemisphere to develop on an agricultural basis." [11]

This may not have come about so quickly if the Portuguese had not experienced almost from the beginning the shattered hopes of their oriental adventure. As João Lúcio de Azevedo wrote, "Neither the pepper of Malabar, nor the gold of Sofala, produced the profit that ambition had imagined during the enthusiasm of the triumphal period. The Crown staggered under the enormous expenses that the maintenance of the empire required, and under the dissipations which those years of fleeting opulence had converted from a custom to a need." [12] The country was in short being drained of its resources and on its way to the bankruptcy that came during the reign of Sebastian. It was, as Azevedo suggests, the awareness of this situation that encouraged the Crown to establish agricultural colonies in Brazil.[13]

The more traditional view is that John III, in order to keep Brazil from falling into the hands of the French, decided to call upon a number of entrepreneurs who would develop Brazil in return for extensive privileges. Actually, the maritime and commercial achievements of the Portuguese have always tended to obscure the essentially agricultural nature of their economy. Bailey Diffie, among others, makes clear how much the sea attracted the Portuguese, and how important their seaborne trade was, but Diffie's seminal little book ought to be read only after one reads Dan Stanislawski's study of Portuguese historical geography.[14]

---

guese and Indians in the Settlement of Brazil, 1500–1580 (Baltimore: Johns Hopkins Press, 1942) .

[11]Celso Furtado, Diagnosis of the Brazilian Crisis (Berkeley and Los Angeles: University of California Press, 1965) , 82.

[12]João Lúcio de Azevedo, Épocas de Portugal Económico esboço de história (Lisboa: Livraria Clássica Editora, 1929) , 241.

[13]Ibid., 242.

[14]Bailey Diffie, Prelude to Empire: Portugal Overseas Before Henry the Navigator (Lincoln: University of Nebraska Press, 1960) ; and Dan Stanislawski, The Individuality of Portugal, A Study in Historical-Political Geography (Austin: University of Texas Press, 1959) .

The raising of sugar cane and the subsequent metamorphosis of cane juice into the traditional sugar loaves demanded a plantation-type industrialized agriculture. The Portuguese had no experience of this kind from their operations at home. Portugal proper was not suited to a plantation economy even with Negro slaves, who began to be imported in sizable numbers from the middle of the fifteenth century. There was, moreover, no tradition of serfdom in a country that had largely escaped the feudal system. Yet the Portuguese Crown was attracted very early to the possibility that the economy might profit from the raising of sugar cane, and at the beginning of the fifteenth century, Italian agricultural experts were brought to Portugal to indicate what could be done. Nothing of a substantial nature was done, really, until after the incorporation of the Atlantic islands, notably Madeira, the Azores, the Cape Verdes, and São Tomé, into the Portuguese space. This was particularly true of Madeira, which by 1493 was already producing 80,000 *arrobas,* or 1,302 tons, per year.[15]

Just as Portugal was able to break the Venetian monopoly of the spice trade, so was she able, in the course of the sixteenth and seventeenth centuries, to monopolize the production of sugar. Primitively, the pre-eminence of Madeira sugar was recognized everywhere, in price, quality, and quantity, but in time the undisputed world producer of sugar was Brazil. When Antonil wrote his *Cultura e opulência do Brasil* some time before 1711, the sugar industry, which had already begun to decline because of competition from the Caribbean islands, was centered in Pernambuco, with 246 *engenhos*; in Bahia, with 146; and in Rio de Janeiro, with 36. Despite the discrepancy in numbers, Bahia, not Pernambuco, was the principal sugar producing area of Brazil, with an estimated annual production of 14,500 cases *(caixas)*. Pernambuco was next, with 12,300. Rio was a close third, with 10,220. Altogether, Brazil produced 37,020 cases of sugar per year.[16] Since each case weighed 35

[15]Azevedo, *Épocas de Portugal Económico,* 229. See also Virgínia Rau and Jorge de Macedo, *O açúcar da Madeira nos fins do século XV Problemas de Produção e Comércio* (Funchal: Junta-Geral do Distrito Autónomo do Funchal, 1962).

[16]André João Antonil (pseud. for João António Andreoni), *Cultura e opulencia do Brazil por suas drogas e minas com um estudo bio-bibliographico por Affonso de E. Taunay* (new ed., São Paulo: Companhia Melhoramentos de São Paulo, 1923), 170–71.

arrobas or about 1,155 pounds,[17] the total production amounted to 42,648,100 pounds or 21,324 short tons.[18] Surely this was not a fabulous production in terms of today's needs, but then, fifty years before André João Antonil published his figures, the population of Brazil was only 184,000 inhabitants, of whom 74,000 were white and 110,000 slaves.[19] When one considers, furthermore, that during the colonial period of about 300 years, the small class of planters exported in sugar alone the equivalent of more than 300,000,000 pounds sterling,[20] it is easy to understand why the greedy Dutch fought the Sugar War over Brazil, from 1624, when they attacked Bahia, until 1654, when they were thrown out of Pernambuco.

To the Portuguese, of course, Brazil rapidly became the land of opportunity, ultimately superseding Madeira, the Azores, and the Cape Verde Islands as sources of wealth. Pero de Magalhães Gândavo, the author of the first chronicle of Brazil, published in 1576, encouraged the poor of Portugal to better themselves by settling in Brazil: "My intention was none other . . . than to point out in brief words the fertility and abundance of the land of Brazil, so that this fame might reach the attention of many people in these Kingdoms who live with poverty, and not doubt about choosing it for their improvement: because the same Land is so natural and favorable to strangers that it shelters and invites all people with betterment, however poor and abandoned they might be." [21] Some fifty years later, Simão Estácio da Silveira again urged the poor of his native country to consider for their improvement the opportunities of Maranhão.[22] Gabriel Soares de Sousa wrote of the wealth of the planters of Pernambuco. More than 100 planters, he said, had in-

[17]In estimating equivalent weights I have largely followed the official Portuguese publication, *Mappas das medidas do novo systema legal comparadas com as antigas nos diversos concelhos do reino e ilhas* (Lisboa: Imprensa Nacional, 1868) .

[18]Antonil, *Cultura e opulencia do Brazil*, 172.

[19]Helio Vianna, *História do Brasil* (2 vols.; São Paulo: Companhia Melhoramentos de São Paulo, 1961–62) , I, 260 *n*.

[20]Roberto C. Simonsen, *História econômica do Brasil 1500–1820*, Brasiliana 100–100A (2 vols.; São Paulo: Companhia Editora Nacional, 1937) , II, 222. See also *Ibid.*, I, 74.

[21]Rudolfo Garcia (ed.) , *Tratado da terra do Brasil, Historia da provincia Santa Cruz* (Rio de Janeiro: Edição do Annuario do Brasil, 1924) , p. 25 of the *Tratado*.

[22]Simão Estácio da Silveira, *Relaçao sũmaria das covsas do Maranhão* (Lisboa: Por Geraldo da Vinha, 1624) .

comes of between 1,000 and 5,000 cruzados; still others, between 8,000 and 10,000. [23] By the end of the sixteenth century, even São Vicente, in the far south, with a less developed economy, had the appearance of "a new Portugal." [24]

Side by side with the cultivation of sugar cane along the coastal regions of the Brazilian East and Northeast went the raising of cattle in the interior. Small farmers, unable to compete with the plantation agriculture of the coastal plains which required large capital outlays, moved inland to take advantage of the Homestead Law (*Sesmarias*). With little or no capital, they were able, often within a short period of time, to join the middle class of cattle ranchers. There were enormous ranches, too, like those of the Casa da Torre,[25] but the traditional *sesmarias* of Portugal, which came to Brazil with Martim Afonso de Sousa in 1530, made it possible for the interior of the country to be settled and thus incorporated into the Brazilian nation.[26] In Antonil's account of Brazil's exports at the beginning of the eighteenth century, the cattle industry, because of the hides it produced, occupied the fourth place, after sugar, gold, and tobacco. Hides even served to wrap the rolls of tobacco which, together with firewater produced from sugar cane, were used by traders to barter for the slaves that were shipped from Africa to the plantation centers of Brazil.[27] In the early days of the gold rush in Minas Gerais, herds from the *Sertão* of Bahia were driven to the mining fields for the sustenance of the miners in the days before the Mineiros themselves turned to agriculture.

If sugar affected in these ways the inevitability of a cattle industry in the *Sertão,* it also had some effect upon the *Bandeiras* of São

[23]Gabriel Soares de Sousa, "Tratado Descriptivo do Brazil em 1587," in Francisco Adolfo de Varnhagen (ed.), *Revista do Instituto Historico e Geographico do Brasil* (Rio de Janeiro, 1851), XIV, 13–365 *passim.*

[24]Fernão Cardim, "Narrativa epistolar de uma viagem e missão jesuitica pela Bahia, Ilheos, Porto Seguro, Pernambuco, Espirito Santo, Rio de Janeiro, S. Vicente, (S. Paulo), etc., desde o anno de 1583 ao de 1590, indo por visitador o P. Christovam de Gouvea Escripta em suas Cartas ao P. Provincial em Portugal," *Revista Trimensal do Instituto Historico e Geographico Brasileiro,* LXV, Parte I (Rio de Janeiro, 1902), 61.

[25]See Pedro Calmon, *História da Casa da Torre Uma dinastia de pioneiros,* Documentos Brasileiros, 22 (2nd ed.; Rio de Janeiro: José Olympio, 1958).

[26]See Costa Porto, *Estudo Sobre o Sistema Sesmarial* (Recife: Imprensa Universitária, 1965).

[27]Antonil, *Cultura e opulencia do Brazil,* 189, 271.

Paulo. For it will be remembered that in their first phase the *Bandeiras* were expeditions to capture Indian slaves. These Indian slaves were preferentially sold in the markets of Rio and the other sugar-producing areas of Brazil, at a time, let it also be remembered, when the union of the crowns of Portugal and Castile, during the reigns of the second, third, and fourth Philips, unleashed the enemies of Spain against Portugal and Brazil and made it more difficult for Brazil to supply itself with slaves from her normal supplier, Africa. The *Bandeiras* lost their momentum when Spain allowed the Indians of the Jesuit Paraguayan missions to be armed. They also suffered when the Portuguese, through their victory over the Dutch in 1648, got Angola back and therefore their principal source of slaves.

By the end of the seventeenth century, Brazil's pre-eminence as a sugar producer was challenged, particularly by the Dutch, French, and English possessions in the Caribbean. It was no longer possible to move the Brazilian crop with ease each year, and increasingly the warehouses of Lisbon were filled with cases of sugar that remained unsold. The advent of mercantilism in France and England naturally led to a preference for their own colonial product, and protective tariffs encouraged the spread of sugar cane in the West Indies. Moreover, the planters of Brazil were not able to keep abreast of technical developments, which further disadvantaged them on the international market.

Gold in enormous quantities was discovered in Minas Gerais during the last decade of the seventeenth century, precisely at a time when the decline in revenues from sugar was beginning to be felt.[28] Later, in 1729, the wealth of the General Mines increased even more with the discovery of diamonds. An excitable Franciscan friar, when writing about riches of this magnitude and of the temptations that they placed in the way of the sinner, took God to task for having wanted to punish Brazil with gold.[29] But punishment or not, gold cushioned the depression that the decadence of the sugar industry

[28]Manoel Cardozo, "The Brazilian Gold Rush," *The Americas*, III (October, 1946), 137 ff.

[29]Frei Apolinário da Conceição, *Primazia serafica na regiam da America* (Lisboa: Na Officina de Antonio de Sousa da Sylva, 1733), 45–46.

had provoked and in 1708 led Francisco Pereira Dantas to explain the economic realities of the day to his colleagues on the Overseas Council:

... in the beginning, when the discovery of gold in Minas Gerais began, we were convinced that the development of these mines was not advisable, because we felt that we risked a stable income, which was that enjoyed by the residents of Brazil as a whole from sugar and tobacco, for an unstable one, which time itself might dissipate, so few assurances had we of the continuity of these discoveries, and that in view of these circumstances we properly ought to discourage and stop them [i.e., the development of the mines], to prevent the depopulation by their settlers of the settled areas of Brazil ....

This attitude, he said, had motivated the allotment of only two hundred slaves to the residents of São Paulo, who were the principal miners, for it was felt "that the impossibility of securing hands to help them mine and cultivate the fields for their sustenance would lead them to give up the work which their diligence and industry had created." Nothing sufficed, however, "to keep them from disemboweling the Rivers of their Treasures"; nor was it feasible "to prohibit the passage of the innumerable people who today live there [in the mining areas] because of the impossibility of closing all means of ingress ...." On the other hand, "experience has shown the great benefits which have accrued to the commerce of this Kingdom and of its Conquests from the development of the said mines ... the fleets which come today [from Brazil] are the richest ... of any other monarch in the world ...." The wealth of Minas Gerais, Dantas added, had given new life to trade, practically paralyzed since the slump of sugar and other Brazilian products on the world market. The great stocks of these articles in the royal customs houses of Lisbon were mute witnesses of the serious plight of Brazilian agriculture. Finally, the acute shortage of money in Portugal was assuaged only by the gold from Brazil.[30]

Many years later Adam Smith was to say what the Portuguese in 1708 thought they knew, that "a prudent law-giver would not wish

[30]Cardozo, "The Brazilian Gold Rush," particularly pp. 159–60.

to encourage gold and silver mining." He went on to say, "Of all those expensive and uncertain projects . . . which bring bankruptcy upon the greater part of the people who engage in them, there is none perhaps more perfectly ruinous than the search after new silver and gold mines." [31] And yet it was gold that populated the region beyond the *Sertão,* that brought prosperity to the maritime cities, and that made it possible for Brazil to make good its claims to areas never dreamed of by the signers of the Treaty of Tordesillas of 1494. Without gold, Brazil would not have received more than 10,000 immigrants from the Mother Country each year, between 1705 and 1750,[32] during that crucial eighteenth century, when Portuguese America was being prepared, however unconsciously, for the adventure of political independence. It was because of Brazil's gold that Adam Smith was able to say (even when his sources of information about Brazil were woefully inadequate) that "no one colony in America is supposed to contain so great a number of people of European extraction." [33]

These people were not only the entrepreneurs who directed the labor that produced the goods exported to Portugal and from there to the rest of Europe; they were also the consumers of Portuguese and other European products that were sold in the stores and warehouses of Brazil. The size of the business between Mother Country and colony was already substantial in Antonil's time. ". . . nobody will doubt," he said, "that Brazil is today the best and most useful possession, for the Royal Exchequer as for the commonwealth, among the several [possessions] that belong to the Kingdom of Portugal, bearing in mind the large volume of goods that each year are shipped from these ports, which are secure mines, and abundantly profitable." [34] On the eve of independence, Portugal received from Brazil such products as sugar, cotton, leather, cacao,

[31]Adam Smith, *An Inquiry into the Nature and Causes of the Wealth of Nations,* ed. Edwin Cannan (New York: Modern Library, 1937) , 529.

[32]Augusto de Lima Júnior, *A capitania das Minas Gerais (origins e formação)* (3rd ed.; Belo Horizonte: Edição do Instituto de História, Letras e Artes, 1965) , 54. In the first edition of his work (Lisboa: Privately Published, 1940) , 32, the author wrote 20,000.

[33]Adam Smith, *Inquiry,* 536.

[34]Antonil, *Cultura e opulencia do Brazil,* 273.

gold, tobacco, coffee, rice, indigo, quinine, sarsaparilla, ipecac, dyewood, lumber, diamonds, firewater, whale oil, and coconuts. From
Portugal, Brazil imported wine, butter, olive oil, brandy, salt, Flem-
ish cheese, vinegar, hams, biscuits, flour, ironware, leather, tin, lead
and other manufactured metals, medicaments, colors, acids, spirits,
paper, books, parasols, furniture, church ornaments, mirrors, glassware, drapes and other materials, cordage, and cotton goods.[35]

The production of sugar declined, it is true, towards the end of
the seventeenth century, and part of the blame must be placed on
the miners' voracious appetite for Negro slaves, which at one time
made it more profitable for the sugar planters along the humid
coastal plains to sell their slaves at the exorbitant prices that they
brought on the open market or move with them to the mining areas,
rather than to use them to raise sugar cane on plantations that were
no longer so productive. There was, of course, the reality of the
world market for sugar, now that the plantations of the West Indies
were in full and efficient production. Brazilian sugar was no longer
able to dominate the market, as it did from 1600 to 1700, [36] or bring,
in every case, compensatory prices. Brazil could have modernized
the industry on a large scale as the Pernambuco and Paraíba Company, following its establishment in 1759, did on a geographically
limited scale,[37] but the newer economic pursuits that resulted from
the Age of Gold proved to be more attractive in the short run than
the profits that might have been expected, in the long run, from an
increase in efficiency through an improvement in the techniques
then employed in the growing and refining of sugar.[38]

The reign of John V, from 1706 to 1750, lived, economically,
under the sign of gold. The abundance of specie gave a false glitter

[35]Adrien Balbi, *Essai statistique sur le royaume de Portugal et d'Algarve, comparé
aux autres états de l'Europe, et suivi d'un coup d'oeil sur l'état actuel des sciences, des
lettres et des beaux-arts parmi les portugais des deux hémispheres* (2 vols.; Paris: Chez
Rey et Gravier) I, 423.

[36]Simonsen, *História econômica*, I, 174.

[37]*Ibid.*, II, 188–89. Adam Smith, *Inquiry*, 542, looked upon the creation of this company as an "absurdity."

[38]Part of the story is covered in C. R. Boxer, *The Golden Age of Brazil, 1695–1750,
Growing Pains of a Colonial Society* (Berkeley and Los Angeles: University of California Press, 1962).

to society and pomp to the civil and ecclesiastical establishments. It is not surprising that the government was hard put to meet the expenses of the King's funeral. The magnificence of John's reign was manifested in Mafra and the Lisbon aqueduct, a marvel of the times and better than anything the Romans had done. He built the baroque library for the University of Coimbra, made the archdiocese of Lisbon a patriarchate, and bestowed upon some of his bastard sons important religious benefices. Not to be outdone by the Most Christian King of France or by the Most Catholic King of Spain, John got the Pope to bestow upon him the title of Most Faithful. But the gold of Brazil, while it contributed to the comforts of Portugal, passed through Portugal as through a sieve, and ultimately who profited most from the gold of Brazil was England.

When, upon the death of King John V in 1750, the man who would later be known as the Marquis of Pombal took over the direction of the affairs of state in the name and at the behest of his master King Joseph I, it was clear that the old order was incapable of giving the country the leadership that it needed. The rise of England and the success of the English in manufacturing, trade, war, and diplomacy stood out in sharp contrast against the backwardness of Portugal. England had become one of the richest nations of Europe, whereas Portugal had become one of the most beggarly.

Adam Smith, with his characteristic biases and his acute sense of observation, attributed the decline to the system of civil and ecclesiastical government that had been foisted upon the Portuguese, the absence of freedom and therefore of experimentation, the restrictions upon trade, the inordinate number of men and women in religious life (to him useless), the laws against the Jews, the protection of privilege, and the like. In Spain and Portugal, he wrote, "industry is . . . neither free nor secure, and the civil and ecclesiastical governments . . . are such as would alone be sufficient to perpetuate their present state of poverty, even though their regulations of commerce were as wise as the greater part of them are absurd and foolish." [39]

It is indeed a point to be argued whether or not Catholicism in a

[39] Adam Smith, *Inquiry,* 509.

country like Portugal was, in the period that followed Trent, a particularly good thing for the economic health of the nation, and
whether or not a less rigid, less authoritarian, and less triumphal
form of Christianity would not have produced better results on the
level of human freedom and human welfare. Certainly the attempt
to make of Portugal an island of purity in the midst of an impure
world, an attempt that occupied so much attention on the part of the
Crown and cost the people so much of their substance, did in time
fail. Perhaps so arrogant an effort to establish a theologically and
philosophically monolithic state should have failed.

During the reign of John V the way was in fact prepared for the
modernization that the Marquis of Pombal was later to attempt.
Not, to be sure, in a substantial manner because that would have
been too much to expect from the courtiers that surrounded His
Most Faithful Majesty, but there were unmistakable signs, nonethe-
less, of the need for change. Father Verney, for example, was John's
pensioner in Rome, where he was influenced by Muratori. Verney
wrote a devastating critique of Portuguese education and of the neo-
Thomistic principles upon which it was based.[40] His critique has the
distinction of beginning the attack in earnest against the Schoolmen
that was to lead to the reform of the University in 1772. When,
during the last years of Pombal's consulate, the last great stronghold
of scholasticism in Europe was overcome and reduced to impotence,
the Portuguese began, at long last, to be introduced to the scientific
revolution of the seventeenth century, from which all the inquisi-
torial powers of Church and State had kept them. When this happened in Portugal, one might confidently say that modernization
was finally on its way.

Pombal changed many things in Brazil and encouraged modernization in many areas of Brazilian life.[41] He did away with the
annual commercial convoyed fleet; he extinguished the state of

[40]Luís António Verney, *Verdadeiro método de estudar*, ed. António Salgado Júnior,
Clássicos Sá da Costa (5 vols.; Lisboa: Livraria Sá da Costa, 1949–1952) .
[41]See especially Visconde de Carnaxide, *O Brasil na administração pombalina
(economia e política externa)*, Brasiliana, 192 (São Paulo: Companhia Editora
Nacional, 1940) ; and João Lúcio de Azevedo, *O Marquês de Pombal e a sua epoca*
(Rev. ed.; Rio de Janeiro: Annuario do Brasil, 1922) .

Maranhão and annexed it to the state of Brazil; he further centralized the administration by abolishing the last of the private captaincies; he moved the capital of Brazil from Bahia to Rio; he abolished the Society of Jesus; he put an end to Indian slavery; he removed the disabilities against the Jews; he curbed the authority of the Inquisition; he reformed the University of Coimbra; he attempted to industrialize Portugal; he established the first public schools in Brazil; he held the Church in check; he attacked the aristocracy and humbled the nobility; and he established monopolistic trading companies and gave them concessions in northern Brazil, hoping by that means to revive the economies of areas that needed reviving. But while he tried to infuse a new dynamism into the society that he directed, he was unable to do it except in an authoritarian manner. It was foreign to his tradition, and to Portugal's, to share authority, and this inability on his part must necessarily have stifled a more generalized dynamism of the kind that he would have wanted. This was the basic paradox, and the tragedy, of Pombal's modernization.

Actually, for all the enthusiasm that they had aroused and the hopes that they had engendered, the reforms of the Marquis of Pombal had not been generally successful. Other palliatives were tried during the reign of Queen Mary I. The Law of 1785 prohibited manufacturing in Brazil, for the benefit of the Mother Country. Scientific missions were sent to Brazil, at a time when "natural philosophy" was the vogue at Coimbra. People like José Bonifácio de Andrada e Silva were sent to study geography and metallurgy in the universities of Europe. And the Royal Academy of Sciences was founded, under the patronage of the Duke of Lafões. With the outbreak of the American Revolutionary War, England turned to Brazil for the cotton and tobacco that she could not so easily get from her American colonies at a time when "the present disturbances," in Adam Smith's understatement, kept England from her natural suppliers. The French Revolution and the rise of Napoleon changed the Western world, and the *ancien régime,* which was, after all, the entrenched regime in Portugal, found itself threatened on all sides. By 1800, as Caio Prado Júnior says, the colonial period had indeed reached a *Ponto morto,* a dead point. It was bankrupt as a system, and it could not, under the circumstances, do more. Providentially for Brazil, John VI arrived upon the scene and, with the good sense that always characterized him, decided that something radically new was needed. That is why he was determined to establish the "Liberal System." The modernization of the nineteenth century would essentially be carried out under this system. But that is another story.

External Factors in the Economic Development of Brazil's Heartland: The Center-South, 1850-1930

Eric N. Baklanoff

THE FORMATIVE PERIOD OF BRAZIL'S ECONOMIC MODERNIZATION, from the middle of the nineteenth century to 1930, can be grasped only in the context of the emerging world economy. Brazil's economic heartland, the Center-South,[1] was initially transformed and shaped by the international commodity, capital and labor markets—the decisive mechanisms in the development of the raw materials producing "export economies."

In sharp contrast to the earlier cycles based on a single export commodity (in which Brazil held a temporary world monopoly), the period under review was characterized by the growth and dissemination of skills and the accumulation of capital per head of population. New production functions were introduced, signifying the substitution of high energy (steam and electric power) for low energy (muscle power of men and animals) converters.

The aim of this chapter is to illuminate the interplay between Brazil's development and the emerging world economy from mid-nineteenth century to the Great Depression. We will analyze in turn the role of the external factors—commodity trade, accumula-

---

[1]The Center-South comprises Minas Gerais and the other seven coastal states to the south of Bahia: Espírito Santo, the state of Rio de Janeiro, the Federal District (Guanabara), São Paulo, Paraná, Santa Catarina, and Rio Grande do Sul.

tion of foreign debt, the immigration current, and direct investments—in the transformation of the Center-South region.

FROM THE UNITED KINGDOM TO THE UNITED STATES: THE WORLD CENTER SHIFTS

The expansion of the South-Center region in its initial phase
was intimately linked with the international economic hegemony of
the United Kingdom. Until the outbreak of World War I, the
United Kingdom was Brazil's leading source of imports, and it supplied the lion's share of foreign capital, both portfolio and direct
investments. As shown in Table II, the United Kingdom's share in

Table I

BRAZIL: INDICES OF ECONOMIC GROWTH, 1880–1929 (or 1930)

Productive Factors	1880	1914	1929 (or 1930)
Population (millions) [1]	11.7	23.7*	37.4
Railway lines [2]	3,400 km.	24,600 km.	32,000 km.
Electric power capacity [3]	negligible	152,000 K.W.*	700,000 K.W.
Value of exports [4]	£ 21,000	£ 65,000	£ 95,000
Foreign capital outstanding [5]	$190 million [6]	$1.9 billion	$2.6 billion

(*) In 1910

Sources:
[1]Ministry of Foreign Affairs, *Brazil: An Economic, Social and Geographic Survey* (Rio de Janeiro, 1940), 35.
[2]*Annuario Estatistico do Brasil*, Ano III (Rio de Janeiro, 1937), 850.
[3]*Ibid.*, 849.
[4]*Ibid.*, 858–59.
[5]Table 2.
[6]In 1880 Brazil's debt in sterling bonds (public and private issues) was £ 39 million. Figures for direct investments are not available. See U.N. Dept. of Economic and
Social Affairs, *External Financing in Latin America* (New York, 1965), 9, Table 4.

the 1914 stock of foreign capital came to roughly 60 percent, or more
than three-fourths of Brazil's external debt and about one-half of
direct investments outstanding. Total British investments in Brazil
in that year constituted nearly one-fourth of the United Kingdom's

overall holdings in Latin America. Thus, Brazil participated in Britain's "Golden Age of Foreign Investment" and became increasingly integrated with the international economy through expanding commodity trade. The impact of British investments and enterprise on Brazil's development has been aptly described by Paul Vanorden Shaw:

> The Santos-Jundiai Railway (now Brazilian), one of the finest in the world, which facilitated the exportation of coffee from the interior of São Paulo via Santos to the outside world and the delivery of seaborne merchandise from Santos up the steep mountain to the capital and interior is an excellent example of the services performed by British capital. The Leopoldina in Rio, railways in the North; ports and docks, flour mills, shoe factories, textile plants, navigation companies, insurance companies, banks, and other activities, many of them pioneers in the economic history of Brazil, confirm the quotation I reproduced at the beginning. British participation was "decisive" in forming the economic structure of Brazil. British business was a constant model which Brazilian business copied or adapted.[2]

Between 1880 and the First World War, Brazil experienced an explosive burst of externally induced investment activity (as revealed in Table I). Foreign capital outstanding increased ten times (from $190 million in 1880 to $1.9 billion in 1914); the railway network was expanded seven-fold (from 3,400 to 24,600 kilometers); electric power was introduced; and the nation's exports more than tripled. A little over $700 million of the foreign capital outstanding in 1914 represented the country's external debt and $1.2 billion comprised direct investments in Brazilian railways, power plants, urban public services, factories, and financial and commercial enterprises.

The movement of foreign capital to Brazil increased its tempo after the turn of the century and averaged $150 million annually between 1909 and 1913; during World War I (from 1914 to 1918) its movement shrank to negligible sums.[3] Remembering that the dollar

[2]Paul Vanorden Shaw "European and Asian Influences in the Economic and Cultural Development of Brazil," *Brazilian-American Survey*, XII, No. 6, p. 42.
[3]*Federal Reserve Bulletin* (August, 1920), 816.

of 1913 commanded a purchasing power more than three times the dollar of the 1960's, we can place the above figures into perspective. That is to say, the value of foreign capital outstanding in Brazil (in today's dollars) reached the massive sum of $6 billion at the beginning of the First World War, while the annual inflow from abroad in the years just cited averaged nearly $500 million!

In the time span between the end of World War I and the Great Depression, foreign capital continued to be attracted to Brazil but with significant changes in country origins. The United States emerged at the end of hostilities as an international creditor nation, reflecting a major shift in the world economic balance in its favor. The position of world banker and leading supplier of development capital was suddenly thrust upon this former bastion of international isolation. The rise of New York as the world's financial center and the relative decline of London helps to explain the ensuing changes in Brazil's foreign investment pattern. United States holdings in Brazil increased by more than $500 million, from $55 million in 1914 to nearly $570 million in 1930, while in the same period Britain's capital investment grew by only $200 million.

From 1919 to 1930 the Brazilian economy (supported by external factors) continued its forward momentum. The nation's railway trackage (as shown in Table I) increased by more than 7,000 kilometers; electric power capacity advanced at an accelerating rate; foreign capital outstanding continued to grow, although at a diminished rate; and exports maintained their upward path, from £65,000 in 1914 to £95,000 in 1930.

While the period between 1880 and 1930 was one of prodigious economic development, it must be remembered that the geographic focus of this development was quite selective. The region mainly affected by the growth-promoting external factors was the Center-South and especially the state of São Paulo. Brazil's incipient industrial establishments were concentrated in the region, as was the nation's agricultural output. The Center-South accounted for 80 percent (and São Paulo state, 43 percent) of the nation's agricultural production in 1926–30 and for an even greater percentage of

Brazil's exports.[4] Also, the massive injections of foreign capital, associated with railway construction and the provision of electric power, were made predominantly in the Center-South. For example, in 1935 three-fourths of the nation's railway lines were distributed within the region, and nearly half of the network was located in two states (Minas Gerais, 24 percent; São Paulo, 22 percent).[5] The Center-South accounted for an even larger share of Brazil's electric power capacity (90 percent) in the following year. The major generating centers were the state of São Paulo (contributing 45 percent of Brazil's electrical capacity), the state of Rio de Janeiro (a little over one-fifth), and Minas Gerais (one-eighth).[6]

Thus from a backward province in 1865, "considered to be of secondary importance, and inferior to those of Pernambuco, Bahia, Rio de Janeiro, and Minas Gerais," [7] the state of São Paulo achieved a position of economic primacy in the 1920's—a position which it continues to hold.

BRAZIL'S EXTERNAL PUBLIC DEBT:
SOURCES AND USES OF LOANS

The collapse of the international capital market during the Great Depression marked the end of over a century of continuous expansion of Brazil's external indebtedness. Foreign borrowing through the issue of bonds guaranteed by the government provided Brazil and other Latin American countries with an important channel of funds for capital formation and development. A country will find it prudent to borrow abroad providing that the net benefit of the loan proceeds (through increments in real national income) exceeds the net cost (the effective rate of interest). The net benefit depends on the real yield on the projects for which the loans are used. The real yield or productivity of a project rests in turn on the availability of

[4]Ministry of Foreign Affairs, *Brazil: Statistics, Resources, Possibilities* (Rio de Janeiro, 1937) , 103.
[5]*Annuario Estatistico do Brasil*, Ano III (Rio de Janeiro, 1937) , 264.
[6]*Ibid.*, 264.
[7]*Facts About the State of São Paulo* (São Paulo: The British Chamber of Commerce of São Paulo and Southern Brazil, 1949) , 12.

complementary factors of production with which the capital is combined. Also, since debt service (interest and amortization payments) must normally be liquidated in the lender nation's currency, the borrowing nation must either increase exports to generate the necessary foreign exchange or substitute for imports.

Brazil apparently had little difficulty servicing its growing external debt even though the effective interest rate on bonds was often very high. Henry William Spiegel points out that sterling bonds (which were first sold in 1824) were issued at an average discount of about 10 percent and dollar bonds (which assumed importance only in the 1920's) at a discount of 11 percent. He estimates that if, in addition to the discount factor, account is taken of commissions, brokerage fees, etc., the actual proceeds from the bonds varied between 80 and 90 percent of their par value.[8] On balance, Brazil probably benefited from its overseas borrowing since "the bulk of the loans went into productive investments such as construction of railroads, port facilities, sanitation and water works, and other instruments of urban improvement." [9] Assuming that the proceeds of the bonds averaged around 85 percent of their par value, it would appear that the effective interest rate on Brazil's external borrowing ranged between 9 to 10 percent. Considering the rapid expansion of the nation's economy and the scarcity of capital, we would be surprised if the marginal value productivity (MVP) of the projects in question did not substantially exceed the real cost of borrowing. The extremely rapid buildup of Brazil's external bonded debt, from less than $200 million in 1880 to nearly $1.3 billion in 1930, was closely associated with the nation's coffee prosperity. Debt could grow and service obligations (interest and amortization) could be met out of the rising exports proceeds. The rising foreign exchange earnings associated mainly with Brazil's coffee exports was one of the essential conditions for successful debt service.

The debt service ratio (the proportion of exports absorbed by in-

[8]Henry William Spiegel, *The Brazilian Economy* (Philadelphia: The Blakiston Co., 1949), 137.
[9]*Ibid.*, 138.

terest and amortization payments) rose gradually from the early 1860's to the latter 1920's:[10]

1861–64	9 percent
1890–92	12 percent
1926–29	15 percent

As Table II shows, Brazil's external bonded debt continued to rise between 1914 and 1930. Of the $550 million increment, U.S. dollar bonds account for $370 million and sterling bonds for a little over $200 million. Brazil's bonded debt to French residents, on the other hand, declined by nearly $50 million. At the close of 1930, then, Brazil's foreign debt had accumulated to a sum in excess of $1.2 billion, as shown below:[11]

(Millions of U.S. dollars)	
Sterling bonds	805
Dollar bonds	374
Franc bonds	62
Other bonds	26
	1,267

A little over a half of the debt outstanding was the direct obligation of the federal government; the balance was owed by the states and municipalities.

Significantly, the political entities which had borrowed the most were all located in the Center-South Region: the states of São Paulo, Rio Grande do Sul, and Minas Gerais; the municipalities of São Paulo, Rio de Janeiro, and Porto Alegre.

FOREIGN DIRECT INVESTMENT

The opening of Brazil to foreign direct investment was closely associated with the organizational efforts of Irineo Evangelista da

[10]For 1861–64 and 1890–92 see Celso Furtado, *The Economic Growth of Brazil: A Survey from Colonial to Modern Times* (Berkeley: University of California Press, 1965) , 175*n*; for 1926–29, see Dragoslav Avramovic, *Economic Growth and External Debt* (Baltimore: Johns Hopkins Press, 1964) , 46, Table 8.

[11]*Annuario Estatistico do Brazil,* Ano II (Rio de Janeiro, 1936) 408.

Sousa, Viscount Mauá, one of Brazil's most celebrated entrepreneurs. The merchant-banker exercised considerable influence over Emperor Dom Pedro II and convinced him of the importance of transportation and immigration in Brazil's modernization.[12] Be-

Table II

FOREIGN CAPITAL IN BRAZIL, 1914 AND 1930
(Millions of U.S. dollars)

	1914			1930		
	External[1] public debt	Private[2] direct investment	Total	External[3] public debt	Private direct investment	Total
U.K.	598	609	1,207	806	590	1,396[5]
France	110	391	501	62	138	200[5]
U.S.	5	50	55	374	194[4]	568
Others	4	146	150	25	450	475[5]
Total	717	1,196	1,913	1,267	1,372	2,639

Sources:
[1]U.N. Dept. of Economic and Social Affairs, *External Financing in Latin America* (New York, 1965) , 16, Table 5.
[2]*Ibid.*, 17, Table 17.
[3]*Annuario Estatistico do Brasil,* Ano II (Rio de Janeiro, 1936) , 408.
[4]U.S. Department of Commerce, *U.S. Investments in the Latin American Economy* (Washington, 1957) , 112, Table 3.
[5]Estimates cited in George Wythe, *Industry in Latin America* (New York: Columbia University Press, 1945) , 154.

tween 1850 and 1870 he promoted the building of railways, ports, and the establishment of textile mills and banks. The participation of foreign-owned subsidiaries and branches in Brazil's rapid economic growth between the middle of the nineteenth century and the First World War was very pronounced. From what must have been a negligible sum in 1850, the value of foreign direct investment outstanding reached a massive $1.2 billion in 1914 (representing a sum of about $4 billion in current U.S. dollars!) . Foreign-controlled businesses in this period played a decisive role in the construction and operation of railways and utilities, and in forging

[12]C. H. Haring, *Empire in Brazil* (Cambridge: Harvard University Press, 1958) .

the vital financial and commercial links between Brazil and the rest of the world.

Foreign enterprise and its associated capital in Brazil represented the extension of the emerging European and, subsequently, American industrial revolutions. Along with direct investments came new patterns of thought and action. In contrast to loan capital, direct investment represents a combination of capital, technology, and management under a single unit of control. Foreign direct investment constitutes a major channel through which the managerial, technical, and marketing skills of industrially advanced nations are made available to less developed economies. As W. Arthur Lewis has suggested, the "craft of managing large enterprises" may well be the foreigner's most important contribution to a modernizing nation.[13] Direct investments from abroad possess a high degree of adaptability: both the management and ownership functions can be substantially integrated with the host country—the first by promoting qualified nationals and the second through the instrumentality of a joint venture. Moreover, the enterprise can expand by reinvesting its earnings in the host country. Unlike loan capital, direct investment does not create a fixed burden of external payment obligations in the form of amortization and interest; profit remittances tend to be flexible and generally vary with the fortunes of the economy.

One-half of the foreign direct investments outstanding in 1914 (see Table II) had originated in the United Kingdom ($609 million) and about one-third in France ($391 million). British holdings were concentrated in railways and public utilities. Also, many of Brazil's grain mills, meat packing plants, and modern sugar mills (*usinas*) in the Northeast were owned and managed by investor groups from the United Kingdom.

The British-owned São Paulo Railway was undoubtedly the decisive factor (together with European immigration flow) in the economic transformation of the state of São Paulo. In 1867, eleven years after a concession was granted to build and operate the railway, British engineers completed the link which joined the port of Santos

[13]W. Arthur Lewis, *The Theory of Economic Growth* (Homewood, Ill.: Richard D. Irwin, Inc., 1955) , 258.

with the city of São Paulo and the interior of the state at Jundiai. The enormous natural obstacles which the builders of the São Paulo Railway had to overcome moved Rudyard Kipling to write: "There must be worse railway country in the world; but I have not seen any. Every yard of those fallacious mountain sides conspired against man." [14] Coffee plantations swept into the new lands opened by the railway, and by 1887 nearly two-thirds of the nation's coffee was grown on the *terra roxa* of the São Paulo plateau.

Direct investments of French citizens were similarly concentrated in Brazilian railways and constituted more than one-half ($267 million) of the total outstanding in 1914. [15] French capital was also invested in port facilities, banking and finance, and agriculture. German direct investments began to attain importance toward the end of the nineteenth century, principally in shipping, trading, and banking.

The economic transformation of Brazil's Center-South owes much to the substantial investments made by the Brazilian Traction, Light and Power Co., Ltd., a Canadian concern with significant British and U.S. participation. The Light Group (as it is popularly called) began operations around the turn of the century and developed the most important electric power complex in Brazil, serving the populous Rio de Janeiro–São Paulo area. Roberto C. Simonsen, the noted Brazilian economic historian, wrote of the Light Group's projects on the São Paulo plateau, in which well-known U.S. technicians collaborated:

> The formation of large lakes on the Coastal Range (Serra do Mar), by damming the rivers running into the interior and the conduction of that volume of water down the mountain side of Cubatão, represents a magnificent achievement which, above all, honors the technicians who conceived it and the engineers who brought about its execution. These constructions gave to São Paulo the possibility of obtaining enough water power to supply three times the size of its present industry, and opened new horizons for other manifold undertakings.[16]

[14]*Facts About the State of São Paulo,* 50.

[15]United Nations, Department of Economic and Social Affairs, *Foreign Capital in Latin America* (New York, 1955) , 52.

[16]*Brazil's Industrial Evolution,* reprinted from the magazine *Brazil Today* and distributed by the Brazilian Government Trade Bureau, 1939.

In addition to the generation and distribution of electric power, the Light Group operated telephone, gas, and intra-urban transportation facilities in Brazil's three most important cities and in smaller localities.

After the end of World War I, foreign direct investments continued to flow into Brazil but with a marked change in country origins. As Table II reveals, British investments remained virtually static; French investments shrank appreciably, from nearly $400 million in 1914 to about $140 million in 1930; U.S. investments advanced sharply (from $50 million to nearly $200 million) ; and investor groups representing the "other" nations increased their equity in Brazil by 200 percent (from $146 million to $450 million). Canadian holdings (estimated at $100 million) and those of European investors other than Britain and France (estimated at $300 million) account for the predominant share of foreign direct investments included in the "others" category for 1930. [17]

United States business firms which had heretofore neglected Brazil in favor of Cuba, Mexico, and Central America became increasingly interested in Brazil as a field of investment during the 1920's. Investments of U.S. subsidiaries and branches flowed into diversified Brazilian activities, mainly public utilities, manufacturing, and petroleum distribution. Belgian investors contributed to the development of Brazil's nascent heavy industry by founding the Companhia Siderurgica Belgo-Mineira in 1921. This firm for a number of years produced the bulk of Brazilian pig iron and rolling mill products.[18]

IMMIGRATION

The migratory current to Brazil accelerated in the 1880's and contributed substantially to the host country's economic transformation. Between 1887 and 1936 Brazil received more than four million immigrants, comprising mainly Italians (1,353,734) , Portuguese (1,147,841), Spaniards (576,825), Germans (154,999) Japanese (177,304) , and Russians (107,170) .[19] Considering that most

[17]George Wythe, *Industry in Latin America* (New York: Columbia University Press, 1945) , 154.
[18]Spiegel, *The Brazilian Economy*, 149.
[19]Ministry of Foreign Affairs, *Brazil: Statistics, Resources, Possibilities,* 36.

of these immigrants had reached their productive years and had acquired some education in their mother countries, Brazil was the recipient of a massive influx of human capital from abroad.

Most of them settled in the temperate areas of the Center-South and began their productive lives as sharecroppers, small independent farmers, craftsmen, artisans, or peddlers. Because of their contact with the more advanced industrial cultures of Europe, they brought new attitudes, new skills, and new perceptions to Brazil. The partially assimilated immigrant population introduced the family-operated commercial farm and the modern system of plowing in southern Brazil.[20] They organized new commercial and industrial enterprises and provided the core of skilled workers and foremen. They and their descendants formed a solid base for a growing middle class; they created an environment in which democracy and industrialization could take root. Emilio Willems, whose definitive work on Brazilian immigration is well known, wrote of the immigrants' special contribution to Brazil's development: "They were also bearers of economic attitudes that were relatively seldom encountered in the old Luso-Brazilian stock. As rural settlers they produced to sell rather than to subsist. As urban dwellers they tended to become entrepreneurs, willing to assume risks and to combine managerial skill with technical knowledge." [21] With the spread of the coffee economy to the São Paulo plateau in the 1870's, the province's manpower shortage became acute. Provincial officials responded by adopting policies designed to attract a large number of foreign immigrants. The policy measures proved successful as the following São Paulo figures indicate:[22]

	Total population	Foreign population
1872	837,000	30,000
1920	4,592,000	834,000

[20]T. Lynn Smith, *Brazil: People and Institutions* (Baton Rouge: Louisiana State University Press, 1963) , 378.

[21]Emilio Willems, "Brazil," in Arnold M. Rose (ed.) , *The Institutions of Advanced Societies* (Minneapolis: University of Minnesota Press, 1958) , 545–46.

[22]*Facts About the State of São Paulo,* 23.

While representing about one fifth of São Paulo's population in 1920, the immigrants (and their offspring) contributed to the state's economic development far out of proportion of their numbers.

The evidence seems pretty strong that it was the immigrants and their descendants who most effectively perceived the industrial opportunities which followed from the coffee prosperity, the railroad boom, and the growth of urban centers. The immigrants were a decisive factor in Brazil's incipient industrial revolution. A sample taken by Willems in 1935 showed that out of a total of 717 São Paulo industrial firms, 521 were owned either by immigrants or by descendants of immigrants.[23] Warren Kempton Dean's study reveals a similar pattern: of a total of 34 São Paulo textile mills in existence in 1917, 27 were immigrant-owned.[24] A more recent investigation by Willems disclosed that, on the basis of random samples taken in 1950, 85 percent of the industrial activities in the São Paulo metropolitan area were in hands of ethnic groups other than Portuguese or Luso-Brazilian.[25] The participation of different ethnic groups in industrial activities included Italians (48 percent), Germans (10 percent), Syrians and Lebanese (5 percent), and others (21 percent), comprising mainly Americans, British, Eastern Jews, and Frenchmen. Similar results are given for the states to the south of São Paulo: in Rio Grande do Sul and Santa Caterina 85 percent of existing industrial enterprises in 1950 were in the hands of immigrant groups other than Portuguese.

THE DYNAMICS OF THE EXPORT SECTOR

Celso Furtado infers that Brazil suffered a downward trend in per capita income in the first half of the nineteenth century so that by 1850 it "had reached a lower point than in the entire colonial era, if the various regions of the country are considered as a

[23]Willems, "Brazil," in Rose (ed.), *The Institutions of Advanced Societies*, 545–46.
[24]Warren Kempton Dean, "São Paulo's Industrial Elite, 1890–1960" (Ph.D. dissertation, University of Florida, 1964).
[25]Emilio Willems, "Brazil," *The Positive Contribution of Immigrants*, (UNESCO, 1955), 133, Tables 23 and 24.

whole." [26] The absence of dynamic economic factors, whether domestic or foreign, held the economy at a low level of equilibrium. Further development of Brazil's economy was blocked by a fundamental market constraint imposed by domestic conditions (extremely low per capita income of its small population) and the inability to expand the sale of sugar and cotton, Brazil's traditional export commodities, in competition with other supplying nations.

The introduction and development of the coffee plant in Brazil provided the thrust for a new era of export prosperity: between the 1850's and 1930 the nation's economy was once again on the ascendant as Brazilian coffee penetrated the world economy through expanding lines of international trade. Through a fortuitous combination of topography, climate, and soil, Brazil quickly attained a comparative advantage in the growing of coffee.

The early coffee plantations were located close to Rio de Janeiro. Transportation by mule convoy set rather severe locational limits and governed that growing areas be located near a port. Also, the coffee enterprises could initially tap the underutilized manpower reservoir which had accumulated in the former mining region. However, with continued expansion of coffee production the surplus of labor disappeared, and inadequate manpower supply thus arose as a major problem in the latter part of the nineteenth century.[27]

In addition to the severe labor shortage, destruction of soil fertility of the land employed in the early coffee expansion further threatened the development of the country's primary export industry. The manpower problem was overcome after the imperial government agreed to subsidize the flow of European immigrants to the Center-South. The problem of soil exhaustion was solved through the construction of railways. The substitution of low-cost steam power for the energy of men and mules opened the possibility of incorporating the more distant lands into the coffee economy. The momentum of Brazil's economic growth was therefore maintained, and accelerated, by the convergence of three external fac-

---

[26]Furtado, *The Economic Growth of Brazil,* 118.
[27]*Ibid.,* see Chap. 24.

tors: the large European migratory current, the foreign capital and technical assistance associated with Brazilian railway construction, and the continuing world demand for coffee.

The center of coffee production thereafter shifted to the São Paulo plateau. Because of the concentration of immigrants in São Paulo, the abolition of slavery in 1888 did not preceptively affect the coffee economy: wage labor had largely supplanted slave labor. Brazil's coffee exports advanced sharply, from 53 million bags (£136,000) in the 1881–90 decade to 140 million bags (£561,000) in the 1921–30 decade.[28] The proportion of coffee in Brazil's total export value fluctuated between roughly one-half and 70 percent during the period 1850–1930, and the nation held a virtual monopolistic position in the world coffee economy. For example, Brazil produced three-fourths of the world's coffee during 1901–15 and about two-thirds during the 1920's.

We have noted that Brazil pursued an externally oriented pattern of development between the middle of the nineteenth century and 1930. In organization and structure, Brazil typified what economists have come to call an "export economy." Such an economy exhibits the following properties: a high ratio of export production to total output in the cash sector of the economy; a concentrated export structure; substantial inflow of long-term capital, including the presence of foreign-owned enterprises; and a high marginal propensity to import.[29] Commonly, in such an economy a large fraction of government revenue is derived from customs receipts. For Brazil, exports constituted the dynamic, autonomous variable which powered the nation's development. The coffee sector was the growing edge of the economy over many decades, but it was also the short-run disturber. The sheer weight of exports in relation to total economic activity dictated that the external market rather than private investment or government expenditure exercised predominant influence on aggregate demand. Because of the highly specialized structure, Brazil relied heavily on foreign sources for many kinds

[28]Ministry of Foreign Affairs, *Brazil: An Economic, Social and Geographic Survey* (Rio de Janeiro, 1940) , 98.

[29]Gerald M. Meir, *International Trade and Economic Development* (New York and Evanston: Harper and Row, 1963) , 5–6.

of consumer and capital goods. In 1913, for example, nearly all of the nation's requirements of iron and steel, coal, and cement came from abroad, and also a large share of the nation's consumption of wool textiles (60 percent), cotton textiles (85 percent), ceramics, glassware, and china (35 percent), and jerked beef (30 percent).[30]

The United States in 1913 had already become Brazil's most important buyer, absorbing one-third of her exports. Germany and the United Kingdom by comparison purchased a little over one-eighth each of Brazil's goods. The United Kingdom, however, was still Brazil's major supplier nation, accounting for one-fourth of her total imports, followed by Germany (supplying 18 percent) and the United States (13 percent). A decade and a half later, in 1928, the United States emerged as Brazil's leading trading partner, purchasing almost one-half of her exports and supplying over one-fourth of her imports.

SUMMARY AND CONCLUSIONS

Brazil's economic heartland, the Center-South region, was initially transformed and shaped by the international commodity, capital, and labor markets. The region offered the natural resources base and unskilled labor; the rest of the world supplied much of the capital, technical know-how, and enterpreneurship.

Foreign capital played a decisive role in the construction and operation of railways, electric power plants, and urban infrastruc ture—and in forging the vital financial and commercial links between Brazil and the rest of the world. Foreign enterprise and its associated capital in Brazil represented the extension of the emerging European and, later, United States industrial revolutions.

The migratory current to Brazil's Center-South region accelerated in the 1880's and contributed notably to the host country's economic and social development. The partially assimilated immigrants introduced advanced technical and organizational methods and thereby raised the nation's capacity to absorb capital and deploy it more effectively.

[30]Frederic William Ganzert, "Industry, Commerce, and Finance," in Lawrence Hill (ed.), *Brazil* (Berkeley and Los Angeles: University of California Press, 1947), 256.

Between the middle of the nineteenth century and 1930 Brazil's economy was on the ascendant, as coffee provided the thrust for a protracted era of export prosperity.

Foreign borrowing through the issue of bonds in world capital markets constituted an important channel of funds for Brazilian capital formation and development. The extremely rapid buildup of the nation's external bonded debt between 1880 and 1930 was closely linked with the international coffee economy. Growing coffee exports (in terms of price and quantity) could be translated into a rising volume of imports and an expanding capacity to service Brazil's overseas debt and effect profit remittances. Thus, exports, borrowing abroad, the inflow of direct investments, and immigration were interdependent and mutually supporting factors. The system rested precariously on the world price of Brazilian coffee.

The preconditions for the Center-South's subsequent industrial revolution—abundant electric power, transportation and communication facilities, labor and entrepreneurial resources, and important urban centers—were largely created during the half century preceding the Great Depression.

The Contribution of Getúlio Vargas to the Modernization of Brazil

John W. F. Dulles

GETÚLIO VARGAS HEADED THE BRAZILIAN GOVERNMENT FROM 1930 to 1945 and again from 1951 until his suicide in August, 1954. A man holding office in those years could hardly have avoided contributing to the changes which affected his country. In the case of Vargas, we see an individual who felt that he had a mission to remake Brazil. Speaking at the new industrial city of Volta Redonda in 1943, Vargas declared the city an example of what was being done to institute "a new mentality in our country." [1]

Before becoming chief executive of Brazil in 1930, Vargas had been an unusually progressive governor of his home state, Rio Grande do Sul, in the far south. He started governing Rio Grande in 1928 after the state had been dominated for decades by conservative "old" Borges de Medeiros. Vargas broke with the past when he established the state bank, with a department to make loans to cattle raisers, and when he brought political unity to the state. He administered under a state constitution which gave great powers to the executive and practically none to the legislature. To his way of thinking this was a useful arrangement.

Vargas took over Brazil after it, too, had long been ruled by an

---

[1]Getúlio Vargas quoted in Morris L. Cooke, *Brazil on the March: A Study in International Cooperation* (New York: McGraw-Hill, 1944) , 56.

ultraconservative regime. He campaigned in 1930 by soberly reading the daring program of the *Aliança Liberal,* which called for a
new election law and such social legislation as allowances for in-
valids and the aged, annual vacations for workers, plus a guaranteed
minimum of nourishment. Had he been elected President in 1930,
he would have had to deal with a Congress controlled by the interests of the large states. His take-over at the head of a victorious
revolution gave promise of breaks with the past.

In this chapter we shall consider contributions wittingly made by
Vargas, and shall mention some aims which he failed to achieve. We
shall consider, also, methods which he used. For the responsible
politician the problem of how to get things done is often greater
than the one of deciding what would be good to do.

CONTRIBUTIONS MADE BEFORE
THE END OF THE ESTADO NÔVO IN 1945

Vargas' best-known contributions to the modernization of Brazil
are those which occurred before the military deposed him in 1945.
He considered these to be component parts of the "new mentality."

Industrial development

Brazil's economy before 1930 was overwhelmingly agricultural
and pastoral. Celso Furtado writes that "the period that began in
1930 must be considered on the whole as the period when the industrial system was implanted." He explains this by writing that "the
political opportunism of the new rulers, far less rigid in their
ideological outlook than the men of Minas and São Paulo who had
formerly governed the Republic, indirectly paved the way for industrialization." [2]

In the effort, which has brought the value of industrial production above that of agricultural production, Vargas personally played
an active role. When he successfully pressed the United States government to finance the foreign currency expenses of constructing

[2]Celso Furtado, *Diagnosis of the Brazilian Crisis* (Berkeley and Los Angeles: University of California Press, 1965) , 100.

the Volta Redonda steel mill, he gave enormous impetus to the program. "The fundamental problem of our economy," he said, "will soon be on a new basis. The semi-colonial agrarian country, importer of manufactures and exporter of raw materials, will be able to meet the exigencies of an autonomous industrial life, providing its own most urgent defense and equipment needs." [3]

After failing to persuade newspaper publisher Assis Chateaubriand to establish a Brazilian cellulose and paper industry, Vargas went to the Klabin firm and insisted. As the late Horácio Lafer of the Klabin firm put it, the Brazilian President got a paper industry for his nation by giving the firm eight days in which to present the plans to him.[4] Vargas also made available the necessary credits at the Bank of Brazil. His government, with some help from Wright Aeronautical Corporation, initiated a national airplane motor factory. He welcomed foreign capital for industry. By 1945, Frederic W. Ganzert wrote, "the country no longer depended on foreign sources for the majority of ordinary articles." [5]

Power

Attention was given to power, essential for industry. Vargas' Five-Year Plan of 1940 visualized developing hydroelectric power at Paulo Afonso Falls in the Northeast, but wartime conditions delayed this work. The extraction of coal, unfortunately low grade, was stimulated in the South. Of greater importance, the first large petroleum discovery was made in Bahia.

Labor matters

The "new mentality"—utterly transforming Brazil from its pre-1930 days—was nowhere more conspicuous than in the field of urban labor.

The regime which was upset by the revolution of October, 1930, had regarded the labor problem as one for the police. When Vargas

[3]Vargas quoted in Cooke, *Brazil on the March,* 55–56.
[4]Interview: Horácio Lafer, São Paulo, August 7, 1963.
[5]Frederic W. Ganzert, "Industry, Commerce, and Finance," in Lawrence F. Hill (ed.) , *Brazil* (Berkeley and Los Angeles: University of California Press, 1947) , 256.

took over in November, 1930, he created two new cabinet minis-tries, one for health and education, and another for labor, industry, and commerce. The latter ministry, called the "Ministry of the Revolution," set to work at once on a paternalistic "New Deal" for urban workers, who then made up roughly 20 percent of the work force.[6] The decree of December 17, 1930, extending pension arrangements, included job protection provisions for those with more than ten years of service.

The system of *sindicatos, federações,* and *confederações,* of work-ers and employers, which is in existence today, was first established in the decree of March 19, 1931, signed by Vargas, Labor Minister Collor, and Justice Minister Aranha.

In 1932 there was a deluge of decrees covering such matters as hours of work, conditions for minors and women workers, and *carteiras profissionais* (identification booklets with employment histories) for all workers. The organization of Labor Justice, with courts for settling labor disputes, sprang from the decrees of May 12, 1932, and November 25, 1932. Two-weeks vacation with pay for commercial and financial workers was decreed on August 19, 1933. [7]

Such decrees and their many successors and amendments were eventually compiled in the huge Labor Code of 1943. For the most part, it has continued functioning until today.

Minimum wages, promised during the 1930 election campaign and mentioned frequently thereafter, became a reality during the Estado Nôvo, the dictatorship which began in 1937 and waned in 1945. The first list of minimum wages, different for different re-gions, was published in 1940 after years of study and long confer-ences between representatives of employers and workers.[8] The same kind of careful study preceded the issuance of the Labor Code of

[6]See George Wythe, *Brazil: An Expanding Economy* (New York: The Twentieth Century Fund, 1949) , 49n.

[7]For a full report on labor legislation, December, 1930, to August, 1933, see Alfredo João Louzada, *Legislação Social-Trabalhista: Coletânia de Decretos Feita por Deter-minação do Ministro do Trabalho, Indústria e Comércio* (Rio de Janeiro: Departa-mento Nacional do Trabalho, 1933) .

[8]Interview: Alexandre Marcondes Filho, São Paulo, August 8, 1963.

1943 and the first increase in minimum wages, made necessary in 1943 by wartime inflation. In addition to establishing minimum wages, Vargas pushed for the establishment of trade schools for the benefit of workers.

Political practices

Before 1930 Brazil was dominated by a small elite who ruled the state political machines in Brazil's two largest states and who took advantage of non-secret and fraudulent voting. This elite also made use of its ability to rule on the credentials of men who claimed to be elected to the federal legislature. Before assuming the provisional presidency in 1930, Vargas condemned these ways, and as governor of Rio Grande do Sul, he even reversed fraudulent elections which had favored his own party. As chief executive of Brazil he was instrumental in making the vote secret, in extending it to women, and in dropping the age requirement for voting from twenty-one to eighteen years. Illiterates, however, continued to be ineligible, as they had been under the Constitution of 1891.

In 1932, when Vargas was establishing the beginnings of Labor Justice, he had experts institute the Electoral Justice system which has lasted until the present. It consists of the Regional Electoral Tribunals and the Superior Electoral Tribunal. Afonso Arinos de Melo Franco considers the Election Code of 1932 one of the most important acts of the Provisional Government (1930–34).[9] But, as he points out, it did not push for the creation of national political parties; and political Brazil, in spite of some class representatives in the 1933 and 1934 Congresses, continued to be heavily influenced by the leading "parties" of a few important states.

In May, 1945, a new electoral code was issued. For the first time in Brazilian legislation, a requirement of political parties was that they be national. In a paper delivered in 1955, Afonso Arinos wrote: "With unimportant alterations," the system decreed by Vargas in May, 1945, "was maintained in later legislation."[10]

[9]Afonso Arinos de Melo Franco, *Estudos de Direito Constitucional* (Rio de Janeiro, 1957), 165–96.
[10]*Ibid.*

Ending the fragmentation of Brazil

The creation of national political parties was a reflection of Vargas' dedication to a larger program which constituted a major contribution. In part, this consisted of forging one nation out of a collection of semi-feudal states run by local party leaders with their own tariff walls, armies, and political machines. Observing the political ways of the mid-1930's and earlier, Getúlio felt that the powers which he persuaded the Army to give him in the authoritarian Constitution of 1937 were necessary to complete this change.

The change began several months before the implantation of the 1937 dictatorship. Vargas and the military ministers, taking advantage of reported, imagined, and invented threats to the nation, succeeded in getting the state troops of important states to take their orders from the federal authorities. This upset governors, and for a while Flôres da Cunha, *caudilho* of Rio Grande do Sul, threatened civil war. When Flôres da Cunha fled to the gambling tables of Montevideo, the first step against regionalism was accomplished.

With the proclamation of the Estado Nôvo in 1937, Vargas and totalitarian-oriented Justice Minister Francisco Campos issued the series of decrees designed to turn the allegiance of citizens to Brazil itself. The state hymns and shields were outlawed, and the state flags were burned publicly in an unusual flag day ceremony.

The effort to have Brazilians think about Brazil was not simply a fight against regionalism. During the short-lived Constitutional Government of 1934–37, Vargas noted that allegiances were being pledged not only to states and their leaders, but also to the sigma of the Integralista Green Shirts and to the hammer and sickle of Communism. Furthermore, some of the colonies of foreigners and their immediate descendants, particularly the Germans and to a lesser extent the larger Italian colony, showed signs of feeling that Brazil counted for little compared with their countries of origin. It was reported that in Rio Grande do Sul there were over 2,800 private German schools, only 20 of which made use of the Portuguese language. Most of Brazil's sixty foreign language newspapers were German and Italian. Editors of the German language newspapers were calling on their readers to support Hitler and to join the local

Nazi political party, until they were prevented from doing so by Vargas. The dictatorship insisted on the use of Portuguese in schools, closed down foreign language newspapers, and ended so many Nazi organizations that the German ambassador became a rude and angry lion who stated that Vargas' drive to Brazilianize Brazil was an affront to the prestige of the great Hitler-run Fatherland. The Brazilian government declared him persona non grata on the day of the Munich Pact.

Vargas likened a new Brazilian legal code to "a single flag," which would protect all Brazilians and provide uniformity.[11] His obsession with unification was reflected in some words he had for the military leaders at the end of 1943. He felt that the inclusion of contingents from every state in the Expeditionary Force which was to fight the Axis abroad was a symbol of this unification.[12]

Attention to neglected regions

Vargas broke with the past when he tried to bring forgotten regions into the orbit of progress, regardless of the origin of the man in the presidential palace. He created federal territories out of areas which state governments were ignoring;[13] he flew around the interior, advertising its good points, and he offered inducements to those who would settle there. His suggested cures for the depressed economies of backward Pará and Amazonas included agricultural colonies, technical steps to improve health conditions, systematic planting, and scientific methods, with which the Instituto Agronômico do Norte was to help.

The job of expanding modern Brazil from the coastal area inward was formidable. Accomplishments were few compared with goals, but a new mentality was helped along by Getúlio.

Aviation

It was natural that in the era beginning in 1930 aviation should have expanded enormously, particularly in so large a nation and

[11]Getúlio Vargas, A Nova Política do Brasil (11 vols.; Rio de Janeiro: Livraria José Olympio, 1938–47) , V, 123.

[12]Ibid., X, 244.

[13]Interview: Juarez Távora, Rio de Janeiro, May 22, 1965; interview: Janari Gentil Nunes, Brasília, October 18, 1965.

one with inadequate land transport. Getúlio, an early enthusiast of air travel, stimulated the expansion. Early in the 1930's he had Eduardo Gomes develop the air mail routes, which were managed by the Army until 1941, when Vargas, over the objection of some Army leaders, created the Ministry of Air. Arrangements worked out between the United States and Brazil just before and during World War II gave great stimulus to aviation. Although the airplane engine factory cannot be regarded a success, other developments had far-reaching effects. These were the acquisition of numerous planes from the United States, and, above all, the construction and enlargement of airports all over Brazil. Between 1941 and 1944 Pan American Airways, working under the Airport Development Program, developed "sixteen landplane and five seaplane bases in Brazil." [14]

Weapons

Telling of the "first lesson" gained by Brazil from World War II, Vargas said in 1944: "Only nations sufficiently industrialized and able to produce within their own borders the war materials they need can really be considered military powers. . . . It should be stressed that the installation of heavy industries, and those which are complementary, has precisely the objective of assuring such a situation for us in the near future, enabling us to manufacture the arms and munitions indispensable for our defense. We are only in the initial phase of this plan of equipment, but what remains to be done will be easily accomplished after the war." [15]

With the Estado Nôvo's existence dependent on the Army, it is not surprising that the acquisition of weapons was at the top of the list of Vargas' goals for building a strong, modern Brazil. Vargas' Five-Year Plan of 1940 called for the importation of fighting planes and destroyers. It also called for fulfillment of the £7,500,000 incompleted portion of the £8,280,000 weapons contract which had been signed in 1938 with Krupp of Germany.[16]

[14]Stetson Conn and Byron Fairchild, *The Framework of Hemisphere Defense* (Washington: Office of the Chief of Military History, Department of the Army, 1960) , 258.
[15]Vargas, *A Nova Política do Brasil*, X, 300.
[16]*Foreign Relations of the United States: Diplomatic Papers, 1940* (5 vols.; Washington: United States Government Printing Office, 1961) , V (*The American Republics*) , 634–35.

By late 1940 the British blockade prevented the further shipment of German arms from Europe. Vargas put pressure on the United States, managing even to get some antiaircraft guns taken from the defenses of New York harbor. "By the end of the war the value of Army wartime deliveries to Brazil under the lend-lease agreement of 3 March 1942 amounted to about $230,000,000 . . . more than twice the total value of all other Army lend-lease deliveries to the Latin American nations." [17]

Administrative reform

By establishing the Conselho Federal do Serviço Público Civil in 1936, Vargas introduced a merit system to determine who were appointed to jobs in the ministries. In 1939 the Conselho was enlarged and made into DASP (Departamento Administrativo do Serviço Público). Under the Estado Nôvo the competitive examination system became the rule in all the ministries and in some of the government-controlled companies. Speaking of Vargas, Luís Simões Lopes, who headed DASP, stated that for the first time in Brazilian history a man in power gave up the political tool of thousands of appointments. By taking the examinations, numerous Vargas foes achieved positions. "This is a silent revolution," Vargas told Simões Lopes as they witnessed the system under which, between 1936 and 1945, 200,000 people took competitive examinations which determined who filled 20,000 posts.[18]

DASP reviewed ministerial budgets, coordinated purchasing by government entities, and did much to provide the administrative efficiency which was called for by the 1937 Constitution. Vargas did not sign decree laws in order to favor friends or influential persons, and Simões Lopes helped Vargas make sure that the decree laws which were issued were in the public interest.

THE PROBLEM OF GETTING THINGS DONE, 1930–45

Before turning to the postwar years, which had their own political characteristics, it might be useful to give a little more attention to

[17]Conn and Fairchild, *The Framework of Hemisphere Defense*, 329.
[18]Interview: Luís Simões Lopes, Rio de Janeiro, December 17, 1966.

what is sometimes ironically called "Vargas' short period of fifteen years" (1930–45). This period was divided into the Provisional Government (1930–34), the Constitutional Government (1934–37), and the Estado Nôvo, or dictatorship (1937–45).

The Provisional Government (1930–34)

Following the take-over by the victorious revolutionaries in 1930, Vargas was assaulted by strong forces which were determined either to depose or to dominate him. There was then no Congress to push for sectional interests, but the pressures were at least as formidable as though exerted through congressmen. Civil war was threatened, and in 1932 the threat was carried out.

Vargas, walking a tightrope between the *tenentes* and the ambitious politicians, was not a military strongman who could simply sign a decree to implement any idea he thought beneficial to his country. The modernization of Brazil, he felt, depended on his continuing tenure, and that tenure required that delicate balances not be upset. Chided for doing nothing in 1932, he pointed out that he was much less free to act than might be supposed. But a good deal was accomplished under the cloak of doing nothing.

Vargas' philosophy was said to be contained in the words *Deixa como está para ver como fica* (Leave things as they are to see how they will turn out). This was less a philosophy than an effective way of dealing with numerous discontented political leaders. Behind a placid, friendly, benign exterior—the face of a man of infinite patience and good humor—lay a mind which was impatient, but which had been disciplined to wait. It was a mind which always probed the future. Impatient at realities which held him back, he never yielded to that impatience.

General Góis Monteiro, speaking of Vargas' Provisional Government in its early stage, described it as unpopular and without any program.[19] American Embassy officials reported that Vargas was fiddling while Rome was burning.[20]

[19]Lourival Coutinho, *O General Góes Depõe* . . . (2nd ed.; Rio de Janeiro: Livraria Editôra Coelho Branco, 1956), 168.

[20]Despatches from American Embassy, Rio de Janeiro, to Washington, March 12, 1931, and April 13, 1931. (In National Archives, Washington.)

The early years of the Provisional Government, however, were the years in which revolutionary labor legislation was enacted and in which electoral procedures were reformed. The Northeast received attention from the federal government such as had been unknown since Epitácio Pessoa, a Northeasterner, left the presidency in 1922. Moreover, in those years Vargas established himself as a political power who could maintain himself, although practically every group which claimed to have made the 1930 revolution had complaints against the resulting government.

Vargas operated more subtly than his predecessors. The spotlight was on the struggle for power—a struggle over which Getúlio quietly presided, genially smoking his cigar and watching contending factions knock each other out. Amidst less publicity, the bases of labor organization and social legislation were established.

The Constitutional Government (1934–1937)

"They have forgotten Brazil," Vargas said of the makers of the 1934 Constitution.[21] In his opinion the modernization of Brazil required a different constitution, one in which a strong, cementing central government would do away with the emphasis on state political machines.

All eyes were on the 1938 presidential election. State assemblies became battlegrounds for deciding who would succeed Vargas. Getúlio, interested in letting the military feel that the usual form of electoral democracy was ruining the country, was assisted by the Communists' attempt to overthrow the regime by force. He was assisted also by the apparent success, elsewhere in the world, of totalitarian governments which seemed inspired by a sense of national purpose.

The Estado Nôvo (1937–45)

Ushering in the dictatorial Estado Nôvo, Vargas told the nation that with moral and political "deceptions" eliminated, the nation could go forward under the new Constitution which he then pro-

[21]Paul Frischauer, *Presidente Vargas* (São Paulo, Rio de Janeiro, Recife, Pôrto Alegre: Companhia Editôra Nacional, 1943), 315.

nounced effective. "Let us restore the nation . . . letting it freely construct its history and destiny." [22]

As this step was backed by the leaders of the armed forces, Vargas was able to deal directly with many issues. Politics required less of his time, and he was in a position to alienate groups for what he felt to be the long-run good of Brazil.

Someone described Vargas as having signed a pact with "the devil," the Army leaders, and it is true that he had to watch his step where they were concerned. For the most part, however, they warmly supported measures taken to end regionalism and to eliminate civilian organizations which were vying with the Brazilian state for allegiances.

The Army leaders' admiration for Axis military might—and, in some cases, their partiality for the Axis—helped Vargas to a certain extent. These were the years in which he was getting from abroad what advantages he could for Brazil. Vargas, an expert at gaining advantages from the conflicts of opposing forces, presided at home over the tug-of-war between Aranha, the Allies' friend, and Dutra, the admirer of the German military. After Hitler violated the Munich Pact by invading Czechoslovakia, Vargas inspected some artillery just received from Germany and made a speech which encouraged the Nazis. The American ambassador concluded that Vargas had decided that Brazil should not place all her eggs in one basket until definitely obliged to commit herself in the event of a world war, and in the meantime should squeeze the maximum out of the United States and the fascist powers.[23]

Vargas' speech of June 11, 1940, aboard the *Minas Gerais*—also encouraging to the Axis—was regarded by his daughter Alzira as an attempt to prod the United States into finalizing the Volta Redonda steel mill financing arrangements.[24] United States diplomats were

[22]Vargas, *A Nova Política do Brasil*, V, 19–32.
[23]Despatch, American Embassy, Rio de Janeiro, to Secretary of State, April 22, 1939. (In National Archives, Washington.)
[24]Alzira Vargas do Amaral Peixoto, "A Vida de Getúlio Contada por Sua Filha, Alzira Vargas, ao Jornalista Raul Giudicelli," *Fatos & Fotos* (Rio de Janeiro) , September 7, 1963.

certainly alarmed at the reports of a "liberal" German offer to finance the mill.[25]

In January, 1941, the chief of the United States Naval Mission to Brazil, A. T. Beauregard, worriedly reported that "Brazil seemed more concerned over future economic independence than immediate preparedness." [26] As late as May, 1941, when the Americans were negotiating an agreement with Brazil about strategic minerals, Vargas wired Hitler: "My best wishes for your personal happiness and the prosperity of the German nation." [27] By then the British blockade had brought an end to the shipment of German arms to Brazil. However, Brazilian Army leaders felt that the fascist powers would win a quick victory in Europe.

In Rio in January, 1942, following the Pearl Harbor attack, Vargas opened the Conference of American Foreign Ministers with a speech which was praised by the Italian ambassador to Brazil because it did not say whether Brazil would, as the United States wished, break relations with the Axis.[28] In it Vargas stressed the importance of economic cooperation. He was, however, about to decide that Brazil should break with the Axis, and he was prepared to use Brazilian popular support of the Allied cause to help him overrule his Army leaders. But there was much that he wanted from the United States. Washington decided that the Export-Import Bank should assist in the creation of Companhia Vale do Rio Doce, the Brazilian government-run iron ore export company. From the United States, Brazil also received arms, financial assistance for railroad improvement, help for the establishment of the airplane engine factory, money for coffee and cacao which could not be

[25]See letter of August 7, 1940, from Acting Secretary of State Sumner Welles to Federal Loan Administrator Jesse Jones, given in *Foreign Relations of the United States: Diplomatic Papers: 1940*, V, 609–10.

[26]Memorandum by A. T. Beauregard (Chief of United States Naval Mission to Brazil) , given in *Foreign Relations of the United States: Diplomatic Papers, 1941* (7 vols.; Washington: United States Government Printing Office, 1963) , VI (*The American Republics*) , 492–93.

[27]New York *Times,* May 10, 1941 (dateline Rio de Janeiro, May 9) .

[28]See letter of January 16, 1942, from Italian Ambassador Ugo Sola to Foreign Minister Osvaldo Aranha, given in Ministério das Relações Exteriores, *Relatório de 1942* (Rio de Janeiro: Imprensa Nacional, 1944) , 120–21.

shipped, and the allocation of scarce United States chemicals and steel products.

In spite of advantages gained by Vargas, the war in many ways set back the modernization of Brazil. Much of the Five-Year Plan had to be forgotten or postponed. Petroleum production had to be deferred. Overstrained railroads, using poor domestic coal, came out of the war in pitiful condition, as did the Brazilian ports. The nation was handicapped by shortages of equipment and fuel.

The Estado Nôvo in 1945

Late in 1944 Vargas pronounced the nation well organized to go ahead.[29] He signed a decree to bring the rural workers of Brazil into the system of *sindicatos*. He believed that he had accomplished much under the 1937 Constitution and that the time was nearing for implementing some of the Constitution's mildly democratic electoral provisions.

In the international field and at home he was foiled. Brazil, he felt, should be one of the leaders in postwar international affairs, and he hoped that the action of Brazil's Expeditionary Force and his own personal relations with Franklin D. Roosevelt might make this possible. Such was Brazil's prestige in 1944 that F.D.R. and top United States diplomats vigorously supported the idea that Brazil have a permanent seat on the United Nations Security Council, together with the United States, France, Great Britain, China, and the Soviet Union. However, the British did not care for the idea; and Soviet opposition doomed this aspiration of Vargas. Soon after, Vargas suffered another blow, the death of F.D.R.

At home the military joined with Vargas' democratic opponents, which left him rather powerless. Encountering strong resistance to his effort to enact an antitrust law, he proposed that the new opposition party, the UDN (National Democratic Union), join him in a "coalition government." The confident UDN declined, however.[30] In the months before the military deposed Vargas, the chief accomplishment was the Electoral Law of 1945. This, forcing political

[29]Vargas, *A Nova Política do Brasil*, XI, 45–50.
[30]Coutinho, *O General Góes Depõe* . . . , 427.

parties to become national, was assailed by the press and the UDN because it came from Vargas.

In reaching the presidency again in 1951, Vargas replied effectively to those who had said that he was "behind the times" because of political views he had expressed during the Estado Nôvo. With Brazil's return to electoral democracy, Getúlio might be said to have been more advanced in practical political ways than his opponents. He noted the ways of Perón in Argentina and spoke enthusiastically to General Góis Monteiro about "the power of the masses." [31] He stressed his nationalism and identified himself with the "poor and the humble"; he spoke against trusts and monopolies. He blamed foreign financiers for his downfall in 1945. [32]

Conditions facing Vargas

The situation was not propitious for getting much done. Nominally, Vargas had a majority in Congress, but it was loath to act. Bills became tied up in committees. Among the many Vargas proposals which died in Congress was his ambitious project for reforming public administration, doing away with needless departments, and creating some new ministries to supervise numerous entities which were reporting directly to the President.[33]

Practically all of the Rio press, remembering the censorship of the Estado Nôvo days, supported the opposition and blamed Vargas for doing nothing. Disenchantment with the regime came rapidly because currency issuances in the last years of the preceding administration brought an upsurge in inflation.

Vargas appreciated that he would be powerless if the working masses turned against him. His opponents, eager to impeach him,

---

[31] *Ibid.,* 439.

[32] New York *Times,* December 1, 1945.

[33] Lourival Fontes and Glauco Carneiro, *A Face Final de Vargas: Os Bilhetes de Getúlio* (Rio de Janeiro: Edições O Cruzeiro, 1966) , 121–22.

would have a field day. But while he sought the immediate ovations required by politics, he tried at the same time to deal constructively with Brazil's future.

The Joint Brazil–United States
Economic Development Commission (1951–53)

This commission, which had the advantage of development studies prepared by the Abbink Mission of 1948, was to recommend the financing of projects, especially those related to transportation and electric power, which would complement private investment and eliminate bottlenecks or promote economic growth. The Brazilian team, headed by Ari Torres, included such experts as Valentim Bouças, Roberto Campos, Glycon de Paiva, Lucas Lopes, and Renato Feio.

On the commission's recommendation the Brazilian federal railways came to be incorporated into one organization, and the National Economic Development Bank was established to handle the financing of the development program.

From a discussion in Washington, the American and Brazilian members of the commission understood that the Washington lending authorities would advance approximately $300 million for the foreign currency needs of approved projects.[34] With this understanding, Finance Minister Horácio Lafer took the unpopular step of increasing taxes in order to raise the cruzeiro requirements, estimated at around the equivalent of $550 million. The commission approved and forwarded to Washington forty-one detailed projects calling for 14 billion cruzeiros in local currency costs and $387,300,-000 in foreign currencies.[35] When Vargas mentioned the foreign currency figure of $300 million on the radio at the end of 1952, the chief of the United States team, Merwin Bohan, was in Washington trying to lay the groundwork for the Joint Commission to bow out in a blaze of glorious goodwill early in the forthcoming Eisenhower

[34]Letter, Merwin L. Bohan (to J.W.F.D.) , December 17, 1963, p. 5.
[35]*The Development of Brazil: Report of Joint Brazil-United States Economic Development Commission* (Washington: Institute of Inter-American Affairs, Foreign Operations Administration, 1954) , 255–81.

administration. With a sense of shock at what he felt to be a lack of good faith,[36] Bohan learned that conditions had changed: Brazil's declining credit-worthiness had come in the way of making the full amount available for the projects approved by the Joint Commission.

After the work of the commission was over, Bohan called on Vargas, who hid well the disappointment he felt at the outcome. Vargas expressed a keen desire "to have all of the work of the Joint Commission published—so that I may deliver a set to President Eisenhower, in order that there be no lack of continuity in carrying out the reciprocal commitments assumed by our two countries." [37]

During 1952 and 1953, foreign currency of $181 million was made available to Brazil for fifteen of the Joint Commission projects, leaving, at the end of 1953, twenty-six projects (calling for $206 million) awaiting action. Although eventually most of the balance came to be provided, the conditions under which the Joint Commission wound up its work contributed to a feeling in Brazil that an unsatisfactory change had been taking place in the United States attitude. Milton Eisenhower, visiting Brazil in July, 1953, did not find Rio's climate friendly. "The Brazilians were furious and made no effort to hide their anger," he wrote.[38]

The Bank of the Northeast

Finance Minister Lafer, visiting the Brazilian Northeast at the time of the 1951 drought, concluded that "in the combat of the *sêcas* up to the present the preoccupation with engineering or hydraulic works frequently overshadows the economic side of the problem." [39] Vargas concurred, and in proposing that Congress establish the Bank of the Northeast, he stated that "in the light of past experience and modern techniques of regional planning, it is time

[36]Letter, Merwin L. Bohan (to J.W.F.D.), December 17, 1963, p. 9.

[37]Interview: Merwin L. Bohan, Austin, August 20, 1964.

[38]Milton S. Eisenhower, *The Wine Is Bitter* (Garden City: Doubleday and Company, 1963), 152.

[39]Horácio Lafer quoted in Stefan H. Robock, *Brazil's Developing Northeast: A Study of Regional Planninig and Foreign Aid* (Washington: The Brookings Institution, 1963), 92.

for a definite economic and social direction to be impressed upon the solution of the problem." As Stefan H. Robock put it, by the time Vargas took the matter up with Congress, "the project had been broadened into a major regional development institution." [40] Vargas signed the law creating the bank in July, 1952.

Petrobrás

In December, 1951, President Vargas submitted his message to Congress asking for the creation of Petróleo Brasileiro, S.A., a state company to extract petroleum.[41] The message makes it clear that he was determined to prevent this industry from falling under the control of foreigners. And yet his proposal would not have ruled out the possibility of some foreign investments in petroleum extraction, nor would it have made Petrobrás a monopoly.

Ex-President Artur Bernardes, a longtime Vargas foe, described Vargas' project as "inspired by the trusts," and he called Vargas "the protector of foreign trusts." UDN congressmen saw the opportunity of appearing more nationalistic than Vargas. In the democratic age no one could be less "patriotic" than anyone else, and the project which Vargas preferred fell by the wayside. Almost everyone in politics, Vargas included, ended up supporting the bill which the UDN took the lead in sponsoring. Passed in 1953, it made Petrobrás a monopoly.

Amapá manganese

In the case of the extraction and exportation of manganese ore from the territory of Amapá, Vargas succeeded in overruling the demands of ultranationalists. The plans for a private company, 51 percent owned by Brazilian nationals and 49 percent by a United States corporation, had been formulated during the preceding Dutra administration. While this proposal awaited Vargas' approval, Vargas was surrounded by ultranationalists who urged that he expropriate the Amapá manganese ore deposits and make them

[40] Robock, *Brazil's Developing Northeast*, 92.
[41] See Vargas' Message to Congress No. 469 of December 6, 1951, and Law Project 1516 of 1951, both given in Câmara dos Deputados, *Petróleo: Projetos 1516/51, 1517/51, 1595/52* (Rio de Janeiro: Departamento de Imprensa Nacional, 1952).

the property of the government of Brazil.[42] By withstanding the "superpatriots" on this, Vargas allowed the creation of a model enterprise, which, besides bringing Brazil badly needed foreign exchange, brought impressive development to once-backward Amapá territory.[43]

Profit Remittances

Vargas often stated publicly that foreign investments in industry were needed. However, in his 1951 year-end political message to a nation which was unhappy about increasing prices, he announced that foreign investors had been "bleeding Brazil" by sending excessive profit remittances abroad "illegally and scandalously." [44] It is true that the remittances had been large, but this was due to the official exchange rate which overvalued the cruzeiros which were used to purchase dollars for remittance abroad.

Vargas and Finance Minister Lafer solved the problem unpolitically. They eliminated the 8 percent ceiling on profit remittances which had been decreed by the Dutra regime, and they established a realistic rate for the cruzeiro. As Eric N. Baklanoff has made clear, these measures helped stimulate a large flow of foreign capital to Brazil.[45] Profit remittances abroad declined, although no longer was there any ceiling on them.

Shunning a radical ultranationalism

José Bonifácio Coutinho Nogueira has described Vargas as being at the same time a demagogue and a conservative.[46] The use of such labels is dangerous in the case of Vargas. But Nogueira's description suggests the importance of judging Vargas on the basis of the decisions he made in his role of chief executive of Brazil. It is reminis-

[42]Interview: Janari Gentil Nunes, Brasília, October 18, 1965.
[43]See Paul Vanorden Shaw, *Know-How Conquers Jungle* (Rio de Janeiro: ICOMI, 1963).
[44]New York *Times,* January 1, 1952.
[45]Eric N. Baklanoff, "Foreign Private Investment and Industrialization in Brazil," in Eric N. Baklanoff (ed.), *New Perspectives of Brazil* (Nashville: Vanderbilt University Press, 1966), 129.
[46]Interviews: José Bonifácio Coutinho Nogueira, São Paulo, November 22, 1965, and December 6, 1966.

cent of a statement by Leonel Brizola, a recent governor of Rio Grande do Sul: "The best advice that I give the people in trying to help them judge their leaders is that the people concentrate not on the words but on the actions of those they follow." [47]

An examination of Vargas' actions reveals a tendency to shun politically attractive ideas of ultranationalists and "superpatriots" which he felt would hardly benefit Brazil. This was as true during the last years as during the earlier Estado Nôvo, when Vargas decided that it would be useful to Brazil to disregard constitutional provisions about nationalizing all banks and sources of hydraulic energy.

Stimulated by Communists, ultranationalism in the last Vargas years became a powerful political factor. The Communists agreed with Artur Bernardes and other Vargas foes who liked to call Vargas the "protector of foreign trusts." Until Vargas committed suicide, the Communists—like some rather conservative opposition politicians—were clamoring for his overthrow. Communists hated the National Security Law of 1953, which was used against them; and they worked hard against the Brazil—United States Military Aid Pact, which was signed by the last Vargas government. They charged Vargas with treason and with being the chief enemy of the Brazilian workers.

With his farewell message, which was aimed at such charges, Vargas came out of it all leaving an image which he thought was more appropriate than the picture drawn by these opponents. After his suicide, the Communists made a complete about-face, identifying themselves and their objectives with his posthumous popularity.

Looking over Communist-inspired placards being waved together with pictures of Vargas early in 1964, one is apt to forget that Vargas had been a chief opponent of the Brazilian Communist Party. Of all the steps which he took against it, perhaps the most effective were the enactment of labor legislation and the establishment of the Brazilian Labor Party; but he also often had his police crack down on Communists.

[47]Leonel Brizola (in *Panfleto* magazine, March 2, 1964) , quoted in Thomas E. Skidmore, *Politics in Brazil, 1930–1964: An Experiment in Democracy* (New York: Oxford University Press, 1967) , 418.

Reading the placards, whose messages were favored by President Goulart and groups of far leftists, one is apt to forget the level-headedness, fondness of balance, and aversion to extremism which characterized Vargas' decision making with respect to the development of Brazil.

A Passion for Equilibrium

In spite of his level-headedness, Vargas was not the emotionless man frequently described in words like the following: "Of all the living statesmen of the world today, Vargas is without doubt the coldest, most rational and cynical. Emotion of any kind he does not know. For him loyalty and consideration have no meaning." These observations were written late in 1937, shortly after Vargas had remarked that "the revolt of creatures against their creators is traditional in Brazilian political life." Vargas had just instituted the Estado Nôvo and gotten himself into a position where he could turn against the fascist-like Green Shirt marchers, whose political support he had recently used.

Vargas subordinated loyalties to particular groups, politicians, regions, or political ideologies to a loyalty to Brazil as a whole. His acts as chief executive, guided by a high sense of responsibility and a deep opposition to financial irregularities, were characterized by this loyalty. This single devotion, combined with a practical mind, makes it difficult to apply the kind of labels which would otherwise define the man's position or ideas.

Conservatives fumed at wage increases decreed by Vargas, the "Father of the Poor." Meanwhile, the leaders of the so-called vanguard of the proletariat called him the "Father of the profit-making sharks." Limeira Tejo puts it well when he describes Vargas as governed by a "passion for equilibrium." [48] When Vargas ruled without a congress he did not exercise power unilaterally, but acted as a rather well-balanced parliament. He felt that his own tenure and the welfare of Brazil both depended on the equilibrium he sought. "My adversaries," Getúlio declared in 1950, "call me Father of the Poor,

[48]Limeira Tejo, *Brasil: Problema de um Continente* (São Paulo: Edições Arquimedes, 1964) , 28.

and Father of the Rich. But I have never been factious or an extremist. Above all, I tried to act justly and to realize the common good. Rich and poor are equally Brazilian." [49]

This was the man who, knowing Brazil intimately, took it from backwardness across a frontier. The Brazil that was left behind had been overwhelmingly agricultural, made up of "arrogant regionalisms, semiconfederate states with their own small local armies." [50] and their own tariff barriers. It had been dominated by a tiny elite who made use of elections which were a mockery, and of a federal congress which, in the words of Cândido Antônio Mendes de Almeida, met "mainly for the purpose of dividing up the budget between the clientele." [51] It was a congress which reflected provincial souls instead of a Brazilian soul.

The new Brazil had more central direction, and it considered economic, political, and social matters from a more national point of view. It had national political parties, a national legal code, and new federal ministries dedicated to labor and industry and to health and education. Brazil, with its devotion to industrialization, its petroleum production and electric power projects, its attention to abandoned regions, and its minimum wages, Labor Law Consolidation, and Electoral Tribunals, was an entirely different country from the pre-1930 Brazil.

Some have said that the changes had to come and that Vargas' chief contribution lay in knowing how to bring them about with the fewest possible shocks. Vargas, the practical nonextremist who liked to make up with former adversaries, was generously endowed with a propensity for using what Tristão de Athayde calls the Brazilian principle of getting things done slowly and in a fraternal atmosphere. But shocks there were—shocks for which neither liberals nor conservatives have forgiven Vargas. All the same, it may turn out that, as Vargas said upon leaving office in 1945, "history and time will speak for me."

[49] Getúlio Vargas, *A Companha Presidencial* (Rio de Janeiro and São Paulo: Livraria José Olympio, 1951) , 215.

[50] Thomas Leonardos, "Palestra Proferida na Escola Superior de Guerra, em 9 de Junho de 1964" (mimeographed speech) , 13–14.

[51] Interview: Cândido Antônio Mendes de Almeida, Rio de Janeiro, December 13, 1966.

The Old and the New in
The Politics of Modern Brazil

James L. Busey

Nem devemos esquecer-nos que sob formas diferentes escondem-se, freqüentemente, impulsos comuns, visando idênticos objetivos.

— Nicia Villela Luz[1]

ON JANUARY 24, 1967, THE CONGRESS OF BRAZIL SAT IN SOLEMN plenary session. Senator Auro de Moura Andrade, president of the Congress, intoned: "In the name of the National Congress which decreed it, invoking the protection of God, I declare promulgated the Constitution of Brazil." [2] There was long applause, and the speaker went on to observe that the new document would go into effect the following March 15, and that all future power was to emanate from the people and be exercised in the name of the people for the benefit of Brazil. Other speeches of eulogy followed.

CONSTITUIÇÕES OUTORGADAS

The new Constitution of 1967 is the creation of a *comissão de juristas,* selected by the President of the Republic. The Congress

[1]Nicia Villela Luz "A monarquia brasileira e as repúblicas americanas," *Journal of Inter-American Studies,* VIII (July, 1966) , 356.
[2]Embaixada do Brasil, *Boletim Especial,* No. 18 (January 25, 1967) .

which adopted the fundamental document had only been elected the previous November 15. Prior to that, forty-six opposition deputies in the previous Congress had been deprived of their political rights and removed from their seats in the Congress; and, during the years from 1964 to 1967, hundreds of other leading figures, including governors, deputies, and three ex-presidents, had undergone a similar deprivation of political rights by decrees of the military regime.[3] On December 1, 1966, the new Congress began deliberations on the proposed Constitution. On December 22, three weeks later, it approved the document by a vote of 200 to 127, with 8 abstentions.[4] From then until January 24, 1967, President-General Humberto de Alencar Castello Branco and others in his administration indicated the amendments that would be accepted and those that would be rejected; and the final promulgation followed, as we have seen.[5]

The Constitution of 1967, in other words, was imposed by the military-dominated regime that had seized power in 1964. We would be quite wrong, however, if we were to assume that this was the first time in Brazilian history that such an event had occurred.

It is true that the constitutional assemblies which drew up the Constitutions of 1891, 1946, and even that of 1934, were composed of representatives from many leading sectors of Brazilian public opinion. The Constitution of 1937, however, was decreed directly by President Getúlio Vargas;[6] and the formation of the imperial Constitution of 1824 offers a most striking parallel to that of the most recent document.

With the cry "Independência ou morte!" Dom Pedro, son of King João VI of Portugal, declared Brazil's independence on September

---

[3]The three ex-presidents were Juscelino Kubitschek, Jânio Quadros, João Goulart.

[4]James L. Busey, *Latin American Political Guide, 1967* (11th ed.; El Paso: Texas Western Press, 1967), 35. It is widely agreed in Brazil that, even if opportunities for meaningful discussion had been more ample, the few days available provided little opportunity for the Congress to make material changes in the proposed constitution. Murilo Melo Filho, "Os últimos 100 dias," *Manchete*, No. 765 (December 17, 1966), 5.

[5]On the attempts by both ARENA and the opposition to propose amendments, see Embaixada do Brasil, *Boletim Especial*, Nos. 237–40, (December 23–28, 1966).

[6]Fernando H. Mendes de Almeida (ed.), *Constituições do Brasil* (São Paulo: Edição Saraiva, 1963), 415–16.

7, 1822. After the coronation of the young prince as Emperor Pedro I, the establishment of a written constitution was the first order of business. The constitutional assembly that met July 3, 1823, included the leading lawyers, clergymen, landed proprietors and military officers of the country.[7] The tendencies of the assembly, as well as of Pedro I, were ostensibly in tune with the liberal spirit of the times; and it seemed that Brazilian constitutionalism could hardly have a more auspicious beginning.

Early in its deliberations, the constitutional assembly took to criticizing the Emperor and to proposing provisions to curtail his authority. Attacks by the assembly upon the proposals of the Emperor became increasingly vitriolic. Finally, November 11, 1823, the troops of Pedro I surrounded the meeting hall, and the Emperor announced the assembly to be dissolved. He stated that tumult and calumny within the meeting made it necessary for him to take this drastic step; that the dissolution of the assembly was essential for the salvation of the country.[8]

After the closure of the Constituent Assembly, Pedro I charged a special ten-member Conselho de Estado with the task of drawing up a new constitutional document.[9] The resulting constitution, which gave more power to the Emperor than had been proposed by the former assembly, was promulgated by Emperor Pedro I and was put into effect on March 25, 1824. One cannot help but note the parallel with the *comissão de juristas,* selected by the Castello Branco regime, which proposed the Constitution of 1967 to the Congress of Brazil.

In the words of T. B. Cavalcanti, the Constitution of 1824 was a *carta otorgada.*[10] According to Dr. Celso Soares Carneiro: "The

[7]C. H. Haring, *Empire in Brazil* (Cambridge: Harvard University Press, 1958), 25.

[8]"Statement of the Emperor on the Dissolution of the Constituent Assembly," in E. Bradford Burns (ed.), *A Documentary History of Brazil* (New York: Alfred A. Knopf, 1966), 205–10; see also T. B. Cavalcanti, *Las constituciones de los Estados Unidos del Brasil* (Madrid: Instituto de Estudios Políticos, 1958), 263; Helio Vianna, *História do Brasil,* II (São Paulo: Edições Melhoramentos, 1962), 79–83; Sérgio D. T. Macedo, *A história do Brasil* (Rio de Janeiro: Edições de Ouro, 1963), 159.

[9]Macedo, *A história do Brasil,* 159; Vianna, *História do Brasil,* II, 83–84; Haring, *Empire in Brazil,* 28.

[10]Cavalcanti, *Las constituciones de los Estados Unidos del Brasil,* xxvii.

Constitution of the Brazilian Empire, despite the democratic principles which it adopted, such as that of the division of the powers of the state and to the effect that sovereignty rested with the nation, suffered from a great defect—it was bestowed *(outorgada)*. That is to say, it was not discussed, voted and promulgated freely by the people, but imposed by the prince. Nevertheless, it was respected and fulfilled during the sixty-seven years of the Empire." [11]

The long life of the Constitution of 1824 is not to be disregarded, and we shall turn to that point in another part of this paper. It is important that we note here that the procedure adopted in formulation of the latest Constitution of 1967 is not new to Brazilian political experience.

EXCEPTIONAL MEASURES

Since the revolution of 1964, the forms and procedures of Brazilian government have been modified drastically by numerous special acts. These have taken the form of four *atos institucionais* and about two dozen *atos complementares,* all of them decreed by the military regime. These, in addition to a very large number of constitutional amendments which the Congress adopted under great pressure, revised profoundly the norms of the Constitution of 1946 well before promulgation of the new Constitution of 1967.

One should not suppose that special, extra-constitutional acts and decrees are unusual to the Brazilian political scene. During the Regency of 1831–40, the imperial regents exercised an alleged authority to revise the Constitution, and decreed an *ato adicional* which provided for elected legislative assemblies in the provinces as well as for reduction of the number of regents from three (as set by Article 123 of the Constitution) to one.[12]

[11]Celso Soares Carneiro (ed.) , *Constituição dos Estados Unidos do Brasil* (Rio de Janeiro: Edições de Ouro, 1962) , 16.

[12]"Lei de 12 de agôsto de 1834," in Mendes de Almeida (ed.) , *Constituições do Brasil,* 68–78. Fr. Diogo Antônio Feijó, an unusual and probably authoritarian figure, was appointed to this post of sole ruler of Brazil and served from 1834 to 1837. See "Feijó Outlines His Political Philosophy," in Burns (ed.) , *A Documentary History of Brazil,* 228–30; and Jacques Lambert, *Le Brésil: Structure sociale et institutions politiques* (Paris: Librairie Armand Colin, 1953) , 118–19.

Even the coronation of Pedro II, which ushered in a golden age of Brazilian political history, violated the strictures of the Constitution of 1824. According to Articles 121 and 122 of that document, the Emperor would remain a minor until the age of eighteen; and during his minority, Brazil would be governed by the Regency. But by legislative act of July 23, 1840, Pedro II was proclaimed to have reached his majority at the age of fourteen; and at fifteen, on July 18, 1841, he was officially crowned Emperor of Brazil.[13] Public demands for termination of rule by the Regency had been accompanied by the cry, "Viva a maioridade de Sua Majestade o Imperador!"

Since that historic day, the legal panorama of Brazil has been sprinkled with *atos adicionais, atos de interpretação,* special *leis constitucionais, decretos* and *decreto-leis, emendas constitucionais* accomplished both by regular and by irregular means, and, during 1964–1967, *atos institucionais* and *atos complementares.* Most of the extra-constitutional devices have appeared during periods of unusual crisis—during the chaos of the Regency (1831–40), the Vargas dictatorship (1930–45), the transformation from dictatorship to constitutional democracy (1945–46), and the recent revolutionary period. If one includes the *emendas constitucionais,* which in many instances wrought sudden and profound changes in Brazilian government and were adopted under the pressures of crisis, one must conclude that no less than seventy-five such unusual and exceptional acts have played their roles in the governmental evolution of Brazil.[14]

Our brief summary makes it clear that the present revolutionary regime of Brazil is not unique, either in terms of its virtual imposition of the Constitution of 1967, or in terms of its utilization of extra-constitutional devices for the governance of the country. Putting the matter another way, one can say that in several stages of

[13]Haring, *Empire in Brazil,* 54–55.

[14]For example, the amendments of September 2, 1961, and January 23, 1963, which instituted and then abolished the parliamentary system. The latter of these was preceded by a national plebiscite, for which there was no constitutional provision. A summary of these extra-constitutional measures may be gleaned from the table of contents of Mendes de Almeida (ed.) , *Constituições do Brasil.*

Brazilian political history, though certainly not uniformly, such utilization of rather irregular tools of political power has been considered a normal feature of Brazilian procedure.

THE ROLE OF THE MILITARY

Nor can it be said to be an altogether new phenomenon that the armed forces should play a heavy role in Brazilian government.

Military campaigns were not an important instrumentality in securing the independence of Brazil, and the military sector seems not to have been a significant element in Brazilian politics until the Paraguayan War (1865–70) strengthened its position. Then, like the Roman armies which fattened upon the demands of the Punic Wars and later destroyed the Republic, the Brazilian military forces began to play a more visible role in the politics of the country.[15]

Soon after the end of the Paraguayan War, crises emerged in relations between the civilian and military sectors of Brazilian society. Particularly in the 1880's, the armed forces took part in a series of disturbances which afflicted the country.[16] The military took to demanding new privileges and perquisites, and were certain that Emperor Pedro II was not giving them the attention they merited.[17] In the words of José Maria Bello: "Sure of the support of the nation's leading class, the Emperor overlooked or slighted the elements that could have reinforced his position—notably the foremost, the armed forces." [18]

During the last years of the Empire, the so-called "military question," which had many ramifications we need not review here, took a leading position in public discussion. The gradual weakening of the monarchy was accompanied by a corresponding flexing of mili-

[15]João Camillo de Oliveira Tôrres, *O presidencialismo no Brasil* (Rio de Janeiro: Edições o Cruzeiro, 1962) , 121–45; José Narino de Campos, *Os grandes problemas do Brasil na década de 60)* Petrópolis: Editôra Vozes Ltda., 1964) , 99; Burns, *A Documentary History of Brazil*, 329; Vianna, *História do Brasil*, II, 194–207.

[16]Haring, *Empire in Brazil*, 135.

[17]Bonifácio José Tamm de Andrada, *Parlamentarismo e a evolução brasileira* (Belo Horizonte: Editôra Bernardo Álvares, S.A., 1962) , 60.

[18]José Maria Bello, *A History of Modern Brazil, 1889–1964* (Stanford: Stanford University Press, 1966) , 9.

tary muscles; then, as Oliveira Tôrres puts it, the Republic was established, and Marshal Deodoro da Fonseca occupied the vacant throne.[19]

Though the Republican Party had carried on active agitation throughout Brazil since 1870, one gets the impression that the armed forces were more responsible than the civilian population for the overthrow of the monarchy of the celebrated Pedro II.[20] The proclamation which ended the Empire and established the Republic gave credit to the military arm by announcing: "Fellow citizens: The people, the army, and the navy, in perfect harmony of sentiment with our fellow citizens resident in the provinces, have just decreed the dethronement of the Imperial dynasty, and consequently the extinction of the representative, monarchical system of government." [21]

The military *golpe* of 1889 set a significant precedent and cast its shadow over the Brazilian political future.[22] The regimes of the first and second presidents, Marshals Manuel Deodoro da Fonseca and Floriano Peixoto, can only be described as military dictatorships.[23] During the first years of the Republic, instances of military turbulence, attempted revolts, and insubordination were numerous.[24] However, with fair elections in 1894, civilian President José de Morais Barros came into office and the militarist threat subsided.[25] But the issue remained very alive in the Brazilian consciousness, and in the heated campaign of 1910 between civilian candidate Senator Rui Barbosa and Marshal Hermes da Fonseca, the question was debated with passion.[26]

[19]Oliveira Tôrres, *O presidencialismo no Brasil*, 145; See also Andrada, *Parlamentarismo e a evolução brasileira*, 57; and Vianna, *História do Brasil*, II, 215–17.

[20]Haring, *Empire in Brazil*, 140–56.

[21]"The Proclamation Ending the Empire," in Burns (ed.), *A Documentary History of Brazil*, 283–84.

[22]E. Bradford Burns, *The Unwritten Alliance: Rio Branco and Brazilian-American Relations* (New York and London: Columbia University Press, 1966), 7.

[23]Cavalcanti, *Las constituciones de los Estados Unidos del Brasil*, xxxvi; and Vianna, *História do Brasil*, II, 226–27, 232.

[24]William Lytle Schurz, *Brazil: The Infinite Country* (New York: E. P. Dutton, 1961), 321.

[25]Haring, *Empire in Brazil*, 169.

[26]Burns, *Unwritten Alliance*, 15–16; and also see "Rui Barbosa and the Issue of Militarism," in Burns (ed.), *A Documentary History of Brazil*, 330–36.

After the hardfisted administration of Marshal Hermes da Fonseca, the civilian sector of Brazilian society played an ascending part in government during the next decade. But during the 1920's, there were the attempted revolts by the *tenentes;* and in 1930 Brazil was introduced to dictatorship by Getúlio Vargas, who was both put into and pushed out of the presidency (1945) by the military arm. He was followed in office by Marshal Eurico Gaspar Dutra; but in 1950, Getúlio was elected to return to the presidency as constitutional incumbent. In 1954, after a lustreless term, Getúlio Vargas was pressured by the military into resigning, which led to his sensational suicide.

In 1955 the armed forces arranged the subsequent political events; and their guarantee assured the inauguration of elected Juscelino Kubitschek on January 31, 1956. The elections of 1960 were also guaranteed by the armed forces. In August, 1961, following the resignation of President Jânio Quadros, it was the military sector which insisted it would not accept the ascendancy of Vice-President Goulart unless his powers were reduced via adoption of a parliamentary system. Afterwards, in the words of Narino de Campos, during 1962–63, various declarations by military leaders served to *aumentar a confusão política.*[27] The army and other military sectors accomplished the overthrow of the government of João Goulart in March and April, 1964. [28] The provisional term of General Castello Branco was followed, March 15, 1967, by inauguration of General Artur da Costa e Silva, who was elected by the Congress by virtue of provisions of an *ato institucional.*

Various writers have propounded the theory that since 1889 the military has substituted for the monarchy as a corrective or "moderating" influence. Gilberto Freyre is emphatic about this, and stresses that it has not been the civilian politicians but rather the

[27]Narino de Campos, *Os grandes problemas,* 101.
[28]See Jordan M. Young, "Some Permanent Political Characteristics of Contemporary Brazil," *Journal of Inter-American Studies,* VI (July, 1964) , 287–301; Narino de Campos, *Os grandes problemas,* 100; and John W. F. Dulles, "Post-Dictatorship Brazil, 1945–1964," in Eric N. Baklanoff (ed.) , *New Perspectives of Brazil* (Nashville: Vanderbilt University Press, 1966) , 28, 33, 44–45, 51–53.

armed forces (and previously, the monarchy) which have always played the role of ultimate constitutional authority.[29]

This very sketchy summary should make it clear that the contemporary participation of the armed forces in the governmental processes of Brazil may have resulted in some unusual forms of governance, but that the leading place of the military sector on the present Brazilian political stage should not be considered as exceptional. It would be more accurate to say that, at least since 1870, the military arm has, except for a few unusual years, stood in the forefront of the Brazilian political process.

AUTHORITY AND PATERNALISM

Observers of the contemporary Brazilian political scene are struck by the combination of democratic forms and heavily authoritarian procedures which have characterized the current revolutionary military regime in Brazil. *Atos institucionais* and *atos complementares* issued directly by the military occupants of the executive branch have ruled, among other things, that (1) revolution is in itself a profound constitutional power; (2) the *atos institucionais* give legality to the Constitution, not vice versa; (3) measures proposed by the President to the Congress must be passed within a limited time or be deemed automatically approved; (4) civil servants at all levels might be dismissed, shifted about, or brought to trial for offenses against the state; (5) political rights of individual Brazilians might be suspended for ten years, thus preventing them from voting, holding public office, or expressing their views in the press; (6) all previous political parties are "extinguished," with new ones to be established; (7) Congress would be elected by direct popular vote as usual, but the new President, Vice-President, and all governors and vice-governors of states would be elected indirectly by the legislative assemblies; (8) the President alone might declare a state of siege, including the shutting down of Congress; (9) the new Constitution of 1967 would be put into

[29]Gilberto Freyre, *New World in the Tropics* (New York: Alfred A. Knopf, 1966), 207–208.

effect according to procedures established in Institutional Act No. 4, which set a rapid succession of dates for its consideration, adoption, and promulgation; and (10) the new Constitution would include certain provisos set forth by decree of Institutional Act No. 4. [30] Most of the provisions of the *atos institucionais* are now a part of the Constitution of 1967, plus authorization to the President to decree *decreto-leis* (subject to ultimate congressional review) on matters relating to national finance and security.[31] The new Constitution sets a fixed time limit of forty-five days for congressional consideration of laws proposed by the President, when he so requests, and of sixty days for consideration of constitutional amendments he submits; and it prohibits congressional action which might raise budgetary appropriations over those proposed by presidential recommendation.[32]

During the last months of his administration, President Humberto de Alencar Castello Branco demonstrated no relaxation in his vigorous administration. On October 21, 1966, he closed down a recalcitrant Congress, and decreed that it could not resume its sessions until December 1, after new elections. Voting for the Chamber of Deputies, November 15, 1966, produced a body wherein two-thirds of the seats were occupied by members of the official party, ARENA. As his administration drew to a close, the President canceled the mandates of several more federal deputies and of various state legislators, municipal *vereadores,* and prefects. He shook up and reorganized the entire command of the armed forces, and brought news commentators to refer to his government as that of *uma democracia forte,* like those of Mexico and France.[33]

The government of Castello Branco was also active in the promotion of social reform.

[30]Busey, *Latin American Political Guide,* 34; and, especially, Embaixada do Brasil, *Boletim Informativo,* No. 69 (April 10, 1964) ; and *Boletim Especial,* Nos. 204 and 225 (October 27, 1965; and December 7, 1966) .

[31]Melo Filho, "Os últimos 100 dias," 4–5; *Constituição do Brasil,* 1967, Articles 54, 58, *et passim.*

[32]Embaixada do Brasil, *Boletim Especial,* No. 204 (November 7, 1966) ; *Constituição do Brasil,* 1967, Articles 51, 54, 60, *et passim.*

[33]Filho, "Os últimos 100 dias," 4–5.

A thoroughgoing land-reform program, which includes land-value taxation, expropriation of unused land holdings, and assistance in colonization, has been approved and is now going into effect. New highways, including one which will connect Callao, Perú, with the port of Santos, are now under construction. The runaway Brazilian inflation, which had reached 144 per cent per year at the end of the Goulart period, has now been slowed down to about 35 per cent, with the expectation that in 1967 the figure will be 15 per cent per year. Economic, banking, taxation, and general fiscal reforms are in progress.[34]

Since April, 1964, then, the governments of Castello Branco and Costa e Silva have ruled with a strong and apparently irresistible hand, but have not been unconscious of social need. Furthermore, freedoms of speech and press, while restrained, have not been restricted in an exceptional or highly authoritarian manner. Recent and current governments of Brazil, in other words, are quasi-democratic, semi-authoritarian, and paternalistic. Furthermore, they are heavily imbued with elitist overtones. These facts of Brazilian life were well underlined by President Castello Branco himself, in his inaugural speech of April 10, 1964. Significantly enough, he quoted from Rui Barbosa, the fiery defender of earlier republican and civilian principles: " 'It is among the more cultured and well-to-do classes that regenerative actions must have their starting point. If we give the example to the people they will follow us.' " [35]

In the commentaries on the Brazilian political process which trace it through the long sweep of history, nothing is more prevalant than this emphasis on paternalistic, elitist quasi-democracy. Gilberto Freyre repeatedly stresses Brazil's monarchical-paternalistic tradition.[36] C. H. Haring points out that under the empire, 90 percent of the population were illiterate, and Brazil was ruled by the privileged social class, mostly *fazendeiros* from the great estates.[37] The persistent paternalistic neo-feudalism that ruled the countryside be-

[34]Busey, *Latin American Political Guide*, 35–36.

[35]Burns (ed.) , *A Documentary History of Brazil*, 383.

[36]Freyre, *New World in the Tropics*. This theme runs through the sociological studies of Gilberto Freyre, and particularly so in his *Casa-grande e senzala* (2 vols.; Rio: Livraria José Olympio Editôra, 1961; and his *Sobrados e Mocambos* (2 vols.; Rio: Livraria José Olympio Editôra, 1961) .

[37]Haring, *Empire in Brazil*, 59.

came the normal mode of political governance and pervaded every aspect of Brazilian life, whether on or off the *fazenda*. Under the Empire, according to the late and distinguished Professor William Lytle Schurz, "the state was an oligarchy of large landowners, as it had actually been during the colony, and no other form was feasible." [38] In his perceptive study of Brazil, Jacques Lambert refers to nineteenth-century Brazil as *une démocratie de notables* wherein "the mass of population and slaves took no part in political life." [39] According to Nicia Villela Luz, the regime of Pedro II was "a constitutional monarchy, yes, even parliamentary with respect to form, but basically a government ruled by a patriarchy, assisted by a council of patriarchs. It was a regime perfectly adapted to the Brazilian society of the times: a society dominated by an oligarchy of the paternalistic type." [40]

The Constitution of 1824 provided for a government that would be unitary, Catholic, and monarchical, under the watchful eye of a strong Emperor.[41] Article 99 of the Constitution stated that the Emperor should be considered both inviolable and sacred. Article 101 provided, among other things, that the Emperor might (1) name the members of the Senate (from lists selected by indirect election), (2) sanction decrees and resolutions of the general assembly, (3) approve and suspend resolutions of provincial councils, and prorogue or postpone meetings of the general assembly (the national parliament), as well as dissolve the Chamber of Deputies as required for the "salvation of the State," (4) freely name and dismiss the ministers of state, (5) suspend judges under certain circumstances, and so on.[42]

These aspects of imperial authority were subsumed under the famous *poder moderador*, which was conceived to be additional to the traditional legislative, judicial, and executive branches of government. In its exercise, the *poder moderador* became so ample that the remaining three functions could not be effectuated without im-

[38]Schurz, *Brazil, The Infinite Country,* 317.
[39]Lambert, *Le Brésil,* 116.
[40]Villela Luz, "A monarquia brasileira e as repúblicas americanas," 364–65.
[41]Cavalcanti, *Las constituciones del Brasil,* xxix.
[42]Mendes de Almeida (ed.) , *Constituições do Brasil,* 23.

perial approval.[43] In writing about the *poder moderador,* students of Brazilian government seldom add that, in addition, the Emperor was responsible for exercise of the *poder executivo.* Article 102 of the Constitution of 1824 placed in his hands a vast detail of powers that flowed from this source. Among many other attributes, the Emperor, acting as executive, could (1) name all the appointees to executive, diplomatic, military, and even ecclesiastical posts, (2) direct all foreign affairs as well as make treaties of all kinds, (3) declare both war and peace, (4) control naturalization of new citizens, (5) issue various sorts of decrees designed to carry legislation into effect, and (6) take all measures relevant to internal and external security. These were not mere *pro forma* provisions for powers exercised in reality by the imperial ministers, as in modern day Britain or Canada. They were actual powers which were in fact undertaken by the Emperor himself.

A most important organ of government was the Conselho de Estado, which served in an advisory capacity in matters of imperial significance and whose members were named for life by the Emperor.[44] This was not the temporary body of the same name which Pedro I utilized to draw up the Constitution of 1824. It was, rather, a permanent and powerful organ of Brazilian imperial government.

Though the Brazilian imperial system was thought to be a parliamentary democracy, the important role of the Emperor modified severely any similarity to the British pattern. Members of the Senate were chosen for life, from triplicate lists drawn up by elected commissions. Disagreements between lower house and Emperor resulted invariably in dissolutions of the former, followed by election of a more tractable body. The Emperor held suspensory veto over all legislation. Furthermore, his cabinets of ministers did not necessarily reflect the political persuasions of his parliaments. Rather, because of imperial control over dissolution and electoral outcomes, the reverse was more often the case. Appointments of ministers were made without reference to parliamentary wishes, and the con-

[43]Soares Carneiro, *Constituição dos Estados Unidos do Brasil,* 16.
[44]Constituição de 25 de março de 1824," in Mendes de Almeida (ed.) , *Constituições do Brasil,* Articles 137 and 138, p. 31; see also Delgado de Carvalho, *Organização social e política brasileira* (Rio de Janeiro: Editôra Fundo de Cultura, 1963) , 177.

cept of cabinet responsibility found little, if any, place in the imperial system. Many decrees in lieu of regular legislation were signed directly by the Emperor, or by the Emperor to the effect that the Legislative Assembly had so decreed.[45] It was for these reasons that the Republican Manifesto of 1870 complained of "omnipotent, perpetual power," and protested that the lower house was "subject to dissolution at the will of the sovereign."[46]

During the Empire, the judicial functions of the realm were turned over to police officials;[47] and Pedro II exercised a strong hand in settling local provincial disputes.[48]

One need not explain to scholars that Pedro II exercised his vast powers with sensibility and restraint, and that he governed in a manner that contributed to the development of democratic experience in Brazil. He was famous for his insistence on modest, democratic conduct by himself and by his associates in government, and it was Henry Wadsworth Longfellow, who came to know Pedro II during the good Emperor's tour of the United States in 1876, who referred to him as a "hearty, genial, noble person, very liberal in his views."[49]

During the years of the Empire, freedom of speech and of the press were respected—perhaps more so than is the case at this moment.[50] But elections were not free and suffrage was certainly far from universal. Only a tiny fraction of the population participated in the vote, and both pressures and fraud were so widespread as to make elections meaningless as indicators of popular will, if such existed. The Emperor has been called "the true Great Elector" and

---

[45]On the signature of decrees, see "The Queiróz Law," 232, and "The Decree Opening the Amazon to International Traffic," 246–47, in Burns (ed.), *A Documentary History of Brazil.*

[46]"The Republican Manifesto," in Burns (ed.), *A Documentary History of Brazil,* 247–51. One may also consult Cavalcanti, *Las constituciones de los Estados Unidos del Brasil,* xxxix; Hernane Tavares de Sá, *The Brazilians, People of Tomorrow* (New York: The John Day Company, 1947), 170; Haring, *Empire in Brazil,* 29, 57, 60, 61; "Constituição de 25 de março de 1824," in Mendes de Almeida (ed.), *Constituições do Brasil,* Articles 10, 11, 13, 40, and 43; and Vianna, *História do Brasil,* 136–39 and 145.

[47]Haring, *Empire in Brazil,* 58.

[48]Schurz, *Brazil: The Infinite Country,* 314–15.

[49]Tavares de Sá, *The Brazilians, People of Tomorrow,* 175.

[50]*Ibid.,* 171.

"the Grand Interventor" [51] and democracy during the nineteenth century, a "façade." [52]

Among Latin American political thinkers of the nineteenth century, the Brazilian monarchy was not considered to be an unmixed evil. Many leaders of Spanish American independence favored a *monarquia paternalista* to prevent disintegration of the social order; and Bolívar, though no friend of despotism, was not an advocate of untrammeled democracy either.[53] The fact seems to be that the Brazilian system managed to legitimize a patriarchal system of society which elsewhere in Latin America lacked the institutions of coherence so essential for stability. In the social context, the Empire performed service for the Brazilian inclinations to quasi-authoritarian paternalism.

Much the same patterns, though not so well defined, prevailed throughout most of the period of the Old Republic. In the words of Charles Wagley, "The early Republic was formally a democracy but was in fact ruled by a small oligarchy." [54] Other authorities write to the same effect and have seen the close resemblance between the actual process of the republic and those of the monarchy.[55] In the words of Gilberto Freyre, the republic "had to imitate the monarchy it had replaced; it had to become somewhat paternalistic." [56] Elections were held, and in some, as in 1910, there were genuine contests; but, in general, the Partido Republicano exercised the *poder moderador,* assigned candidates and won all the elections from 1894 to 1926. This pattern remained unchanged until a dissident candidate, Getúlio Vargas, overthrew that order of things

[51]Cavalcanti, *Las constituciones de los Estados Unidos del Brasil,* xxx.

[52]Munhoz da Rocha, *Presença do Brasil* (Rio de Janeiro: Livraria José Olympio Editôra, 1960), 118 and 124; Sílvio Gabriel Diniz, "Quatorze anos de eleições na Vila do Pará, Minas Gerais (1861–1875)," *Revista brasileira de estudos políticos,* No. 17 (July, 1964), 144–45; Cavalcanti, *Las constituciones de los Estados Unidos del Brasil,* xxx; Haring, *Empire in Brazil,* 110; Bello, *A History of Modern Brazil,* 23.

[53]Villela Luz, "*A monarquia brasileira e as repúblicas americanas,*" 361.

[54]Charles Wagley, *An Introduction to Brazil* (New York and London: Columbia University Press, 1963), 251.

[55]Burns, *The Unwritten Alliance,* 2.

[56]Freyre, *New World in the Tropics,* 203–204.

in 1930.[57] When he came to power, Vargas did move far from any of the usual Brazilian pretensions to democracy;[58] but he remains an extremely popular figure in Brazilian political folklore, and he was responsible for the introduction of a vast program of social legislation. Vargas was far from democratic. Much of his rule, however, was not disharmonious with the paternalistic traditions of Brazil. Professor Jordan M. Young claims that Brazil can only be said to have practiced real democracy during the period 1945–64. [59]

During most of the nineteenth century, the Emperor invoked the *poder moderador*. In the old republic, 1889 to 1930, either the Republican Party or the military forces, or both, exercised this function. From 1930 to 1945, Getúlio Vargas, with the military never far in the background, filled this traditional role in Brazilian life. Today, one cannot but agree with Professor E. Bradford Burns when he says that the military officers of the republic have taken over the functions of the *poder moderador*.[60]

Gilberto Freyre, while admitting the important role which has been played by Brazilian paternalism, regrets its influence. It is his judgment that it has "made Brazilians too much dependent upon paternalism and paternalistic government." [61] In the sense of maintenance of stability, if nothing else, Professor Jordan Young may be right when he says that "Brazil has been best governed by strong chief executives." [62] Many would consider it regrettable that the total structure of Brazil has not been more conducive to a successful marriage between democracy, order, and progress.[63]

[57]Haring, *Empire in Brazil*, 170; and Juarez R. B. Lopes, "Some Basic Developments in Brazilian Politics and Society," in Baklanoff (ed.) , *New Perspectives of Brazil*, 59–77.

[58]See Getúlio Vargas, *A nova política do Brasil* (Rio de Janeiro: José Olympio Editôra, 1938 and 1940) .

[59]Young, "Some Permanent Political Characteristics of Contemporary Brazil," 290–91. For a study of the difficult role of the legislative branch in the Brazilian context, see Rosah Russomano de Mendonça Lima, *O poder legislativo na república* (Rio de Janeiro and São Paulo: Livraria Freitas Bastos, S.A., 1960) .

[60]Burns (ed.) , *A Documentary History of Brazil*, 380.

[61]Freyre, *New World in the Tropics*, 202.

[62]Young, "Some Permanent Political Characteristics of Contemporary Brazil," 292.

[63]For problems of Brazilian stability, see James L. Busey, "Brazil's Reputation for Political Stability," *Western Political Quarterly*, XVIII (December, 1965) , 866–80.

OTHER ELEMENTS

Several incidental elements of the present Brazilian political scene are no more unusual than are the features of imposed constitution, exceptional measures, military dominance over politics, or quasi-authoritarian paternalism, which we have discussed to this point.

Parties

During the Empire, the Conservative and Liberal parties alternated in office as seemed appropriate to the purposes of the Emperor and in conformity with the wishes of the ministers. As we have seen, election results were dictated more by considerations of imperial policy than by popular demand at the polls. Bonifácio de Andrada tells us that the parties hardly existed outside the parliament, and that only the Republican Party, after its emergence in 1870, had what one might call some attachment to the grass roots and carried on energetic political activity.[64] In provincial assemblies some real party battles occurred, and epithets were hurled in bitterness and anger;[65] but in terms of general public opinion, these were highly divorced from the popular scene; and elections could be manipulated to reflect the imperial judgment respecting the national interest of Brazil.

During the Old Republic, as we have seen, the Liberal and Conservative parties disappeared and power remained in the hands of the Republican Party. Candidates were determined by deals among party leaders and generally rotated between the states of São Paulo and Minas Gerais. In fact, it was the dissatisfaction of the *mineiros* with nomination of a second successive *paulista,* Júlio Prestes, that led to the successful revolution of 1930 by *gaucho* (Rio Grande do Sul) Getúlio Vargas. Vargas proclaimed Brazil to be a state without parties, but near the end of his dictatorship his followers founded the Partido Trabalhista Brasileiro and the Partido Social Democrático; and his opponents founded the União Democrática

[64]Andrada, *Parlamentarismo e a evolução brasileira,* 61.
[65]Diniz, "Quatorze anos de eleições . . . ," 184–91.

Nacional. For eighteen years after 1945 these and numerous minor parties competed for the popular vote. Many writers have commented on the fragility, artificiality, and elitist control which characterized Brazilian parties during this short period.[66] Programs defied definition, and political contest was more related to personalities than to any sort of meaningful political ideas or programs.[67]

By Ato Institucional No. 2 of October 27, 1965, the regime of General Castello Branco declared all political parties to be "extinct," and arranged that new parties might be formed under electoral laws to be promulgated by the government.[68] Subsequently, the supporters of the revolutionary military government formed the Aliança Renovadora Nacional, or ARENA; and opponents organized the Movimento Democrático Brasileiro, or MDB. Since that time, many of the members of the MDB were deprived of their political rights; but the party continues a precarious existence and holds about one third of the seats in the Congress. The attachments of the general population to either of the two parties may be as tenuous as were those under the Empire, or under the Old Republic or the New, but further research is needed to clarify this point.

Federalism

The Constitution of 1967 provides that the former Estados Unidos do Brasil is to revert to its original and simpler name, Brasil. Though the forms of federalism are to continue, the central government is granted huge authority with respect to intervention and control over matters relating to the states. There can be little doubt that the Brazilian pendulum is swinging back to a less federal and more unitary type of territorial distribution of powers.

Brazilian federalism has had an irregular career. The Constitu-

[66]Wilson Figueiredo, "A indefinição dos grandes partidos," *Cadernos brasileiros*, V (May-June, 1963), 3–7; Busey, "Brazil's Reputation for Political Stability," 872–74; Carvalho, *Organização social e política brasileira*, 218–32; and T. Wyckoff, "Brazilian Political Parties," *South Atlantic Quarterly*, LVI (Summer, 1957), 281–88.

[67]See also Dulles, "Post-Dictatorship Brazil, 1945–1964," in Baklanoff (ed.), *New Perspectives of Brazil*, 9; Schurz, *Brazil: The Infinite Country*, 318; Lourival Fontes, *Política, petróleo e população* (Rio: Livraria José Olympio Editôra, 1958), 23, 27, 30, 33, 36.

[68]Embaixada do Brasil, *Boletim Especial*, No. 204 (October 27, 1965).

tion of 1824 placed centralized power in the hands of the Emperor and his government.[69] Both during the colonial and the imperial periods, geographical reality, if not constitutional precept, awarded a certain amount of autonomy to some of the stronger provinces, and this pattern continues to this day in such states as São Paulo, Minas Gerais, Guanabara, Rio Grande do Sul, perhaps Bahia, and a few others.

Under an Ato Adicional of August 12, 1834, a larger scope of autonomy was granted to the provinces, thus laying the groundwork for development of later forms of federalism.[70] But all through the period of the Empire, there could be no doubt of the centralized authority of the imperial government.

The Constitutions of 1891 and 1946 established theoretical federalism, but several of their articles granted so much power to the central government as to raise serious questions as to the areas wherein state government might exercise its authority.[71] Brazilian federalism was highly imitative of U.S. practice but with the additional Brazilian feature that national intervention in state affairs was common—usually for political rather than for national reasons.[72]

From 1937 to 1945, during Getúlio Vargas' so-called Estado Nôvo, federalism was abolished. The dictator ruled by decree, whether in matters affecting state authority or not, and he shifted governors and other state officials in and out of office at his pleasure.[73]

Machado Horta reports that during most of her history, Brazil has been governed under a system of *federalismo centralizador*.[74] With-

[69]Haring, *Empire in Brazil*, 29; see also "Constituição de março de 1824," in Mendes de Almeida (ed.) , *Constituições do Brasil*, Articles 98–104, 165, 166, et passim.

[70]Soares Carneiro, *Constituição dos Estados Unidos do Brasil*, 17.

[71]See Constitution of 1891, Articles 1–15, 34–35, 48, 63–67, et passim; and Constitution of 1946, Articles 5–35, 65–66, 87, 145–65, 166–75, et passim.

[72]Raul Machado Horta, "Problemas do federalismo," in Raul Machado Horta and others, *Perspectivas do federalismo brasileiro* (Belo Horizonte: Universidade de Minas Gerais, 1958) , 11–46.

[73]T. Lynn Smith, *Brazil: People and Institutions* (Baton Rouge: Louisiana State University Press, 1963) , 566–69.

[74]Horta, "Problemas do federalismo," 41. For an outstanding study of Brazilian federalism, see João Camillo de Oliveira Tôrres, *A formação do federalismo no Brasil* (São Paulo: Companhia Editôra Nacional, 1961) .

in the states, *municípios* have been traditionally dominated by the leading families and their *donos,* and it is these powerful figures who have comprised the *câmaras* of the *municípios.*[75] There, at the roots of Brazilian social paternalism, may be found the seeds of many of the features of government we have discussed.

Cancellation of Mandates

During the period of Castello Branco, 1964–67, observers of Brazilian politics were struck by the introduction of devices for cancellation of mandates of legislators—that is, their removal from office by decree of the regime.

Before the congressional election of General Artur da Costa e Silva, October 3, 1966, the political rights of forty-six opposition members of Congress were suspended, which amounted to cancellation of their authority to serve in the Congress. It was a truncated Congress which then elected Costa e Silva to the presidency, a post which he occupied on March 15, 1967.[76] The cancellation of mandates seems to have been unnecessary and self-defeating, because the final vote was 295 in favor of Costa e Silva's election, with 170 abstaining. Had all the opposition members been in the Congress, there would still have been a safe margin in favor of General Costa e Silva; and the military regime would have been spared the uproar of denunciation which ensued. In the end the pandemonium of criticism within the Congress became so great that on October 21, President Castello Branco decreed that it be recessed until after new elections of November 15. [77] By this action the regime unleashed a new storm of denunciation against itself. General Costa e Silva, the official candidate, had been elected but with each new act of the government the victory became more Pyrrhic.

During the Empire, of course, the General Assembly was dissolved whenever the Emperor thought it necessary in order to harmonize its views with those of the ministers he had appointed, and this occurred no less than forty times. In addition, Pedro I dis-

[75]Smith, *Brazil,* 561.
[76]Busey, *Latin American Political Guide,* 34.
[77]Embaixada do Brasil, *Boletim Especial,* No. 195 (October 21, 1966) .

solved the constituent assembly in 1823, as we have seen, and simply closed down the General Assembly in 1824. Upon proclamation of the Republic in 1889, all legislative mandates were canceled. President Deodoro da Fonseca dissolved the Congress in 1891. The same occurred when Getúlio Vargas overthrew the Constitutional government in 1930, and again, in 1937, when Vargas dissolved the Congress and proceeded to rule by decree.[78] Though Brazil has known previous collective cancellations of legislative mandates, it must be confessed that individual, selective cancellations are new. It may be, in fact, that this is the single political innovation contributed by the post-1964 revolutionary governments.

Indirect Elections

A favorite device of current regimes has been to choose the President, Vice-President, governors and vice-governors by indirect election—that is, by the Congress or by the state legislatures, as the case may be. By "authority" of an *ato institucional,* this arrangement was used in selection of President Costa e Silva and in the choice of present state governors. In the more sophisticated form of a large electoral college consisting of members of the national Congress and of delegates chosen by state legislative assemblies, this has now been incorporated into the new Constitution of 1967 for selection of the President.

Though indirect election of executive heads was not known to any previous republican constitution, the concept is not entirely new to Brazil. In fact, during most of the period of the Empire, the indirect election of all members of the national General Assembly played a very important role in Brazilian politics. According to Article 90 of the Constitution of 1824, nominations of deputies and senators, as well as of members of provincial councils, would be accomplished by indirect election. Electoral colleges would be chosen by the people in *assembléias paroquiais.* The electoral colleges, in turn, would name national deputies and provincial legislators, as well as draw up triplicate lists of senatorial nominees, for

[78]News items, *Manchete* and other sources, during October, 1966.

final selection by the Emperor. In the words of Sílvio Gabriel Diniz: "The voters chose the members of the Council (*Câmara*) of the town (*vila*), the district judges of the peace and the electors. It fell to the electors to choose the provincial deputies, the national deputies, and the senators, as the case might be.[79]

The post of *eleitor* was regarded as highly important, and leading clans within the provinces vied for the honor and influence which were associated with it. The *eleitores* constituted a sort of political elite, not only because they were likely to be among the most influential *donos* of the country, but also because their electoral duties added another dimension to their prestige and power. The imperial wishes usually prevailed in the deliberations of the *colégios eleitorais*, and though fraud and pressure were rampant, there were meaningful electoral contests.[80]

Direct elections were established in 1881.[81] But the concept of indirect election was not forgotten; and after proclamation of the Republic, provisional President Deodoro da Fonseca ordered the governors of the states to provide lists of electors, who would in their turn choose deputies to the constitutional convention which was to draw up the Constitution of 1891.[82] Since that time the idea of indirect elections lay dormant until resurrected by the present revolutionary regime for selection of executive rather than legislative officials.

Instability

By comparison with most of her Spanish American neighbors, Brazil has enjoyed periods of relative calm—as, for example, during the reign of Pedro II, during a portion of the Old Republic, and during the shorter republican period of 1946–64. At such times, writers have tended to interpret all of Brazil's political history as being one of tranquil, stable constitutional government. Other re-

[79]Diniz, "Quatorze anos de eleições . . . ," 145.
[80]See *ibid.*, 146. Tabulations of certain elections in the Vila de Pará, Minas Gerais, 1861–75, pp. 173–84.
[81]Haring, *Empire in Brazil*, 111.
[82]*Ibid.*, 167.

search has already questioned this position, and it would belabor the point to unnecessarily dwell on the matter here.[83] A few words will suffice.

Any Brazilian schoolbook is full of accounts of the almost innumerable disturbances which have wracked the country, even in the early years of the Empire.[84] Riotous conditions during the Regency (1831–40) almost tore the nation asunder and were responsible for the early declaration of the majority of Pedro II, age 14, and his precipitate coronation as Emperor.[85] The symbols of monarchy, as well as the able rule of the great Pedro II, brought political peace to Brazil, and the last revolt under the Empire was suppressed at Recife, Pernambuco, in 1849.[86] With the inauguration of the republic, disturbance broke out again, and there were but few years during the period 1891–1930 which can be said to be entirely without overt or covert uprisings, military insubordination, or rumblings thereof.[87]

In connection with the various aspects we have discussed, we have already reviewed the confused conditions of Brazilian political life which accompanied recent events, such as the beginning and end of the Vargas dictatorship, the later suicide of Vargas, the election of Kubitschek, the irresponsible resignation of Quadros, his replacement by Goulart, and of course the revolution of 1964.

[83]In Busey, "Brazil's Reputation for Political Stability," there are citations on various sides of the question of Brazilian stability.

[84]See, for example, Mário da Veiga Cabral, *História do Brasil: Curso Superior* (29th ed.; Rio de Janeiro: Livraria Francisco Alves, 1959), which is almost a chronicle of internal uprisings, military insubordination, attempted *golpes*, and the like.

[85]Burns (ed.), *A Documentary History of Brazil*, 230–31; Vianna, *História do Brasil*, II, 104–22.

[86]Haring, *Empire in Brazil*, 58.

[87]On this point, Bonifácio de Andrada in his *Parlamentarismo e a evolução, brasileira*, 66–77, provides a most useful listing of such threats to the Brazilian constitutional order, including depositions of governors, revolts, extra-legal imprisonments, general insurrection throughout the country, acts of sedition, riots, federal interventions in the states, mysterious deaths of important politicians, states of siege, agitations and demonstrations, known assassinations, civil war in localities, states, and regions, outright revolutions, revolutionary attempts by Communists and Integralists, sudden and unexpected crises endangering the foundations of government, and general domestic strife.

All the republican constitutions of Brazil, as well as that of the empire, have included ample provisions for suspension of constitutional guarantees and declaration of state of siege, a power which now lies substantially with the President of the Republic.[88] During the republic, such declarations and suspensions occurred on twelve different occasions prior to 1964. During 1891–1964, a period of seventy-three years, different parts of Brazil (though not the entire country) have been in state of siege for a total of 3,106 days, or the equivalent of almost nine years.[89]

CONCLUSION

Seen in the broad sweep of her political history, the patterns of Brazilian governance fall into a format which is somewhat different from that which seems to emerge with this or that peculiar set of circumstances. We can conclude that many features of the current period, which may have seemed unusual when seen only in the light of the Brazilian political system during 1946–64, are in fact well known through the long range of Brazilian experience, and can be found to have recurred in a rather persistent manner throughout the years of Brazilian political evolution. A diagram of government types which can tell us a great deal about political systems throughout the world can be so arranged as to place anarchy and tyranny at the two opposite extremes, zero and tenth degrees, and stable constitutional democracy between the two, at the fifth degree, but also at the opposite end from either anarchy or tyranny. On such a scale, it would not be inaccurate to show Brazil as oscillating between about the third and seventh degree, in this manner:[90]

[88]See Constitution of 1824, Article 102, Sec. 15; Constitution of 1891, Article 6, No. 3; Article 34, No. 21; Article 48, No. 15; Article 80; Constitution of 1934: Article 91, Sec. I–a; 175; 178, No. 4; Constitution of 1937: Article 74, Sec. K; 166–73; Constitution of 1946: Article 5, Sec. III; Sec. XIII; 206–15; 217, No. 5; Constitution of 1967: Articles 152–56.

[89]Biblioteca da Câmara dos Deputados, "Estado de Sítio," *Revista brasileira de estudos políticos,* No. 17 (July, 1964), 193–210.

[90]For further clarification of the conceptual scheme behind this diagrammatic form of political representation, see James L. Busey, "Political Terminologies Revised," *Social Studies* XLVI (November, 1955), 257–59.

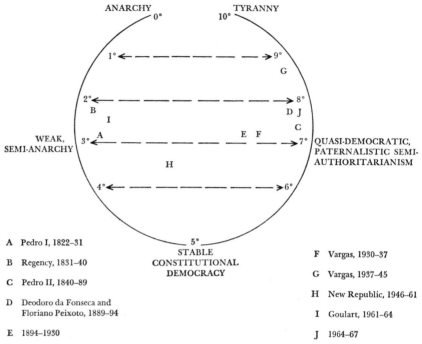

A   Pedro I, 1822–31

B   Regency, 1831–40

C   Pedro II, 1840–89

D   Deodoro da Fonseca and
     Floriano Peixoto, 1889–94

E   1894–1930

F   Vargas, 1930–37

G   Vargas, 1937–45

H   New Republic, 1946–61

I   Goulart, 1961–64

J   1964–67

With these facts in mind, it is important that we design some hypotheses which may be of aid to the analysis of the broad scheme of paternalistic quasi-authoritarianism and constitutional irregularity which have been characteristic of Brazilian government and politics. It is obvious that the paternalistic features of *fazenda* life pervade Brazilian society and politics, and we have already stressed that point. Here, some further application to the political scene is appropriate.

The concept of the *poder moderador,* which was first expressed in the Constitution of 1824, provides us with a most significant tool for understanding Brazil's political features as well as her constitutional irregularities and disturbances. During the Empire, the *poder moderador,* as a mediating but ultimately authoritarian device, was overtly expressed in the Constitution itself. Pedro I and the Regency handled the *poder* very clumsily; but Pedro II, a man of great talent and among the most cultured and able monarchs of his time, understood the paternalistic nature of his society. He ruled with a magnificent insight which is the ideal of the aristocratic concept, though only rarely achieved in fact. He exercised his great authority with restraint and served his people with an honor and dignity that brought from them and from the whole world a degree of respect which discouraged intrigue and revolt.

In his interesting volume, *The Evolution of Brazil Compared With That of Spanish and Anglo-Saxon America,* which was based on lectures which he delivered at Stanford in the autumn of 1912, Manoel de Oliveira Lima expressed these seminal thoughts:

> ... the maintenance on the throne of the traditional dynasty represent-ing the Portuguese past, whose heir, however, identified himself with the new destinies of the country and even made himself the decisive agent of its independence, not only removed the crown of Brazil from the conflict of ambitions, but gave the national traditions a strength and importance unique, compared with what occurred in the neighboring countries of the new Spanish world. ... For many reasons, the Brazilian monarchy in the nineteenth century may be said to have been the politi-cal régime truly suited to the social status of Latin America.

> Thus it was that it succeeded in representing, in Latin America, do-mestic peace and liberty at a time when a condition of anarchy prevailed in nearly all the rest of the continent.[91]

The reign of Pedro II was quasi-democratic, quasi-authoritarian, elitist, and paternalistic. Pedro II was a strong ruler, but he was a good, generous, and honorable ruler. He was the neo-feudal lord par excellence.

As we have seen, the Republic turned the *poder moderador* over to the *Partido Republicano* and the armed forces. The governments under the Republic acted with some authority, and their acceptance by the public depended in large measure upon the abilities of the successive presidents. Disorders reappeared on the Brazilian scene and continued to plague the government to the time of Vargas. From 1930 to 1945, Vargas alone took on the mantle of the *poder mod-erador*. His rule was highly authoritarian, and from 1937 to 1945 it became capricious, unpredictable, and disoriented from any

[91]Manoel de Oliveira Lima, *The Evolution of Brazil Compared With That of Spanish and Anglo-Saxon America* (New York: Russell and Russell, 1966) , 117.

regular patterns of law. The orderliness of rulership which had been a feature of the government of Pedro II was not in the land, and government by *decreto-lei* led to the overthrow of the Vargas dictatorship; but Vargas did institute a great program of social reform, with legislation designed to benefit labor and the underprivileged, the forgotten little people of Brazil. As a dictator unbridled by the regularities of the law, Getúlio Vargas undermined his own chances of political survival, but as a good father to his people, as a worthy patriarch and *dono,* Getúlio remains to this day the most popular figure in the recent political history of the nation.[92]

After the Vargas dictatorship, the new republic stumbled along through eighteen years of both progress and confusion, and it was hard to know what had happened to the *poder moderador*.

Now, there is no question. The *poder moderador* has been assumed by the armed forces of the nation. Despite many blunders, the regimes of President-Generals Castello Branco and Costa e Silva have exercised power with a combined reliance on authoritarianism in fact and democracy in form which could not but remind the observer of parallel aspects of the governments of Pedro I and Pedro II.

The other side of the good Brazilian ruler, as we have seen, is that he must be generous with his people, with *o povo.* He may rule without close attention to all the niceties of democracy, but he had better not forget the needs of the populace. He can be a strong political *fazendeiro,* though it is better that he also be a good one. He must be merciful and generous with *o povo.* The paternalistic attribute of service to the people was a feature of the Empire, of some of the administrations under the old republic and most of those under the new, and was certainly a predominant characteristic of the Vargas dictatorship. The vigorous program of social reform undertaken by the Castello Branco regime and presently being continued by that of Costa e Silva, indicates that current governments intend to follow the same path.

[92]Freyre, *New World in the Tropics,* 204, attributes this phenomenon to the paternalistic attentions which Vargas showered upon his people.

Other writers have pointed to the importance of the popular masses in the Brazilian political scene,[93] and we need not expand on the point here. Nor is it our purpose to try to predict the fate likely to befall the current political arrangements.

It is our conviction that the "best" form of government is that of constitutional democracy, wherein the maximum possible numbers of people enjoy individual rights and freedom of choice, security under the rule of law, and meaningful participation in decision making, during the maximum possible time.[94] The record of all such governments everywhere attests to their success as instruments for the betterment of their citizens; and the dismal record of governments by sheer force is a living testimony to their failure.

But what is "best" for Brazil may not be feasible at the present time or in the foreseeable future. If our findings have merit, it would seem that a *feasible* government for Brazil would be one which, like those of Pedro II, of Rómulo Betancourt of Venezula, of José Batlle y Ordóñez of Uruguay, of Ricardo Jiménez or Cleto González Víquez of Costa Rica, of Benito Juárez of Mexico, or of several others of Latin America, would be strong and good, effective and generous, quasi-authoritarian and honorable, and would pursue the great aim of preparing political and social Brazil for democracy, for the acceptance of freedom without paternalism, for the understanding of self-government.

It was our able director, Dr. Eric N. Baklanoff, who stated that a "unique but modified 'Luso-tropical heritage', combined with creative leadership" should contribute to the favorable development of Brazil.[95] These words were well chosen. Political Brazil is still the creature of the economic and social paternalism which social historians have noted repeatedly.

[93]Lopes, "Some Basic Developments in Brazilian Politics and Society," 67.

[94]James L. Busey, *Latin America: Political Institutions and Processes* (New York: Random House, 1964, 1965) , 8.

[95]Baklanoff (ed.) , *New Perspectives of Brazil*, 300.

Postwar Brazilian Industrialization: Growth Patterns, Inflation, and Sources of Stagnation

Don Huddle

BRAZIL'S POSTWAR INDUSTRIALIZATION IS AN EXAMPLE PAR EXCELlence of outstanding success followed by dismal failure. Between the years 1949 and 1961, "real" national product increased by more than 5 percent annually and industrial output by more than 10 percent annually; but after 1962 per capita output has remained almost constant while industrial output has actually declined up to 1966.[1] This reversal is not just a temporary "recession," the causes of which will tend to recede naturally after a time, but is inextricably tied to numerous longer run forces—the emergence of serious bottlenecks in the social overhead capital sector, in regional and sectoral incomes, and in exports; the spiraling inflation; an imbalance between the industrial and agricultural sectors; and finally the deep involvement of the federal government in price controls and protection subsidies to industry.

The present paper has two purposes: First, to determine the sources and structure of the postwar industrialization; Second, to examine and then reinterpret the characteristics of Brazilian postwar growth. The following section summarizes several widely held characterizations of the Brazilian industrialization "model." Though disagreeing on certain specific details, these "models" have been

[1]Calculated from data of Fundacao Gétulio Vargas, Rio de Janeiro, Brazil.

broadly similar. In Part III is undertaken the difficult task of measuring the form of growth in the dynamic sector—manufacturing—which serves as the basis in Part IV for an evaluation of previous interpretations of the industrialization. The final section attempts to set out a stylized reinterpretation of these events, including the effects of governmental policies, dualism, and imbalances in the economy.

Interpretations of the Industrialization

Previous models of the rapid industrialization in Brazil focus attention on the roles played by (1) inflation-induced forced saving; (2) import substitution; (3) the sluggish international demand for Brazil's exports (predominantly primary products); and (4) foreign investment. At the most general level, the model of Brazilian industrialization has been loosely as follows:[2] The government has been committed to a high rate of growth for the economy. However, expansion of export earnings did not permit the target rate of growth to be achieved in a normal pattern, so the country turned to import substitution to reach its goals. Import-substitution industrialization required the government to tinker with the exchange system and expand credit to the industrial sector. An increased rate of inflation necessarily resulted both from the reduction of wage and salary (consumption) goods as a proportion of total imports (for which are substituted capital and intermediate inputs), and from an expansion of loans to the industrialists. Income stabilization of the coffee sector accelerated the inflation, but was not its sole cause. The inflation, however, was not harmful to the industrialization, but actually favored it by redistributing income from the consuming classes (wage and salary earners) to investing classes (entrepre-

[2]Principal works on which the model is based are: Werner Baer, *Industrialization and Economic Development in Brazil* (Homewood, Ill.: Richard D. Irwin, 1965); Celso Furtado, *Diagnosis of the Brazilian Crisis* (Berkeley and Los Angeles: University of California Press, 1966); United Nations, "Fifteen Years of Economic Policy in Brazil," *Economic Bulletin for Latin America*, IX, No. 2 (November, 1964) 153–215; United Nations, "The Growth and Decline of Import Substitution in Brazil," *Economic Bulletin for Latin America*, IX, No. 1 (March, 1964), 1–61.

neurs). Only when wage and salary earners were able to keep up with the price increases did the inflation become destructive. However, the disappearance of price-wage lags is not believed to have been the sole growth-dissipating factor. Although Werner Baer, for instance, seems convinced that the lag was important, he places more emphasis upon both political problems and social imbalances as the causes of stagnation after 1962.[3] Celso Furtado, on the other hand, sees the price-wage lag disappearing in the late 1950's,[4] but he also stresses political bottlenecks, the numerous errors he believes the authorities made in selecting infant industries for subsidies and protection, and the worsening external terms of trade.[5] The Economic Commission for Latin America cites a host of bottlenecks, including the lack of sufficient domestic demand and the increasing harm done by longer term absolute protection of industry.[6]

Several quotations from the literature highlight the key elements in the general "model." For example, Furtado explains inflation's role as follows:

During the last three decades, industrialization has persistently been supported by the convergence of . . . two factors: substitution for imports, and transfer of resources caused by inflation.

. . .

Inflation is a process of redistributing income, variously caused by always operating for the benefit of groups linked to investment.

. . .

Inflation played a major role in raising the investment rate and concentrating investment in the industrial sector. Without inflation, the rate of growth would certainly have been lower.[7]

The crucial role played by inflation also occupies a central place in Baer's interpretation: ". . . the inflationary process is a natural

[3]Baer, *Industrialization and Economic Development*, 198–201.

[4]Celso Furtado, "Political Obstacles to Economic Growth in Brazil," *International Affairs* (April, 1965).

[5]United Nations, "The whole problem . . . lies in the fact that the restrictions in absolute terms should not last too long," Economic Bulletin for Latin America, IX, No. 1 (March, 1964), 51.

[6]United Nations, "The Growth and Decline of Import Substitution in Brazil," 255–56.

[7]Furtado, *Diagnosis of the Brazilian Crisis*, 101, 103, and 104, respectively.

concomitant of a country which faces continuously declining import earnings, which is committed to a high rate of growth, and which meets its external situation by promoting import-replacement industries and new export industries. The function of the inflationary process is to force the consuming sector to save in order to reduce imports replacements. . . . A lag in wages and salaries is . . . a sine qua non for making the inflationary process a productive one." [8] He goes on to state that inflation did play a positive role in Brazil without having an obviously negative effect on social productivity.

But the inflation eventually lost its virtues according to Furtado: "From the moment when the terms of trade began to deteriorate the only remaining source that could feed inflation without provoking a spiral of prices and costs was lost. The government had to abandon the taxation of exports implicit in the difference of exchange rates, and cover the lack of reserve funds by further emissions of paper currency. Thus, inflation ceased to be an effective mechanism for the redistribution of income, and more and more became simply a sterile game of passing the buck." [9]

Judgments regarding the pattern and desirability of the industrialization differ. Baer is probably most laudatory:

Because of the type of protectionist policies encouraging verticle integration, fairly well balanced industrial growth took place. Industries with high linkages were stimulated, and the linkages worked themselves out through the economy. This explains the rapid spread of the industrialization which resulted . . . with industry becoming the principal contributor to the gross domestic product. . . . Policy measures which accompanied protectionist actions produced an industrialization of considerable depth . . . so that in a short period of time most manufactured products were almost entirely produced within the country.[10]

Furtado and the Economic Commission for Latin America do not disagree with the notion that Brazil had to follow an import-substitution industrialization model, but each stresses errors made in its implementation:

[8]Cf. Baer, *Industrialization and Economic Development in Brazil,* 115.
[9]Furtado, *Diagnosis of the Brazilian Crisis,* 107.
[10]*Ibid.,* 149.

A lack of a consistent policy of industrialization was the concentration of investment in "less essential" industries. The less essential a product the more difficult was its import . . . therefore, sectors producing luxury goods had the greatest attraction for investors. In contrast, the development of the capital goods industry was delayed. . . . investments in infrastructure and the basic industries (iron and steel for example) was allowed to lag behind badly . . . the economic system was badly unbalanced showing excess capacity in some sectors, and inadequate capacity in others . . . to maintain a reasonable degree of ultilization of productive capacity, demanded the raising of the level of expenditure (consumption plus investment) well above that of the income generated by domestic production, a process which is possible only by incurring a substantial margin of foreign indebtedness.[11]

On the same subject the Economic Commission stated that "the crux of the problem is not the impossibility of continuing with substitution, but the fact that the series of incentives created have virtually lost all of their power. . . . the strategic problem confronting the Brazilian economy is to make the transition from an import substitution model to a self-sustaining growth model. . . . Only the public sector . . . is capable of providing autonomous demand on a sufficient scale to counterbalance the negative effect of the exhaustion of the external stimulus." [12]

THE CONFIGURATION OF THE INDUSTRIALIZATION

In the present section the sources and patterns of manufacturing product growth—*the* dynamic sector in the postwar period—are analyzed for the period 1948 to 1963. Events were far from homogeneous during this epoch; wars, changes in leadership, and many other elements produced complex new relationships in the socioeconomic-political areas. We attempt to reduce heterogeneity by subdividing the 1949–63 period into three more homogenous periods (1949–53; 1953–58; and 1958–63) in which growth patterns, rates of inflation, and policy instruments used by the government were less dissimilar.

[11]Furtado, "Political Obstacles to Economic Growth in Brazil," 255.
[12]United Nations, "The Growth and Decline of Import Substitution in Brazil," 57.

In what follows, output growth patterns and growth sources are analyzed for each of the subperiods. The brunt of the discussion relies on empirical findings in four tables. Tables I–III show calculations of the rates of output growth, and the proportion of imports and domestic production, respectively, to the total supply of manufacturing goods. Table IV is taken from a detailed series of estimates I made elsewhere and summarizes the *sources of growth* of consumer, intermediate, and investment goods sectors between: (1) domestic demand; (2) import substitution; and (3) export demand. By discovering where new production was utilized in the economy, we can decide how important import substitution was in postwar Brazilian growth as compared to domestic demand and export demand. These findings do not imply cause and effect relationships, however; they only demonstrate what occurred ex post. An interpretation of the causal relationships between policies and events is postponed until the final section.

The First Subperiod: 1948–53

Following severe wartime shortages in Brazil which affected the structure and level of production and trade, the government adopted policies which bordered on laissez faire.[13] Foreign exchange restrictions were dissembled, banking controls loosened, and other encumbrances on economic life eased. This happy state of affairs did not last long, however, for the government had greatly underestimated the liquidity of the private sector and its desire to spend on imports at the highly overvalued cruzeiro-dollar exchange rate. Thus, the large stock of gold and foreign exchange reserves accumulated during the war was quickly dissipated and the authorities began to reinstitute and progressively tighten exchange control and credit.

Though the coffee boom was in full force, foreign exchange shortages persisted. But, due to the Korean War, import restrictions were nevertheless relaxed; by 1952 the remaining exchange re-

---

[13]Cf. Donald Huddle, "Balances de Pagamentos e Controles de Cambio no Brazil," *Revista Brasileira de Economia*, Fundacao Getulio Vargas (March, 1964) , 6–40, for a detailed description of Exchange Policies during these years.

serves were exhausted and an astounding short-term foreign debt was added. Inflation also became a major policy issue once again by the end of 1953 as domestic prices accelerated in response to a rejuvenation of import restrictions, increased government spending, and a precipitous jump in wages and salaries. The minimum wage, for instance, more than doubled in January, 1952. [14]

Tables I–IV provide the basis for the following observations: The growth rate of product in manufacturing industry fell relative to the 1939–48 period annual average. In addition, import substitution was more than nominal in only the investment and related goods sector, while in the consumer goods and intermediate product industries import liberalization (negative substitution) occurred. Export demand was an insignificant source of growth in all sectors. In summary, this was the period of slowest growth and structural change in the postwar years prior to 1962.

The Second Subperiod: 1953–58

Policy instruments were more uniform and exogenous shocks less important than during any of the previous periods. The government undertook a relatively systematic program of subsidies-taxation and protection designed to promote rapid expansion of selected industrial sectors. Moreover, it undertook to provide added social overhead capital for industry in general. Inflation continued, but not beyond the limit which could be considered as uncontrolled or dangerous. [15]

The growth rate of industrial production accelerated relative to the previous period. For the first time, import substitution became a source of growth in every sector, even consumer goods which regained earlier losses caused by import liberalization. With several individual exceptions, export demand played a very small, though

---

[14]IBGE (Instituto Brasileiro de Geografia e Estatistica), *Anuario Estatistico,* 1962.

[15]Wholesale price increases fluctuated from 25 percent in 1953 to 3 percent in 1957. Cost of living increases were less volatile and slightly higher than wholesale price increases. Data source: *Conjunctura Economica* (March, 1964).

positive, role. Domestic demand, on the other hand, remained the prime source of expansion for all sectors.

The Final Subperiod:1958–62

Policy instruments of the previous period still predominated, and yet several important changes affected the economy. The first of these was the all-out drive for foreign capital investment intimately connected to the ambitious program to establish an automobile industry within several years. Although in 1955, Instruction 113 gave numerous concessions to foreign capital, foreign participation in the economy became most significant just prior to and during the present period.[16] Numerous concessions were made in the way of guarantees, favorable exchange treatment, etc. By 1963, however, foreign investment had fallen to the low levels of the early 1950's. Second, the rate of inflation dangerously accelerated. At the same time the resignation of President Quadros and the appearance of numerous social and economic imbalances raised questions of political and social discontent.[17] By the end of this period, almost all of the factors favorable to expansion seemed to dissipate as indicated by: (1) accelerating inflation without forced saving; (2) disincentives to foreign investment; (3) stagnant export earnings; (4) social unrest and demands for drastic reforms; and (5) weak and vacillating leadership.

Although the overall rate of growth in industry increased, the growth of several sectors which had been instrumental in leading the expansion during the previous period perceptibly slowed; expanding sectors were mainly those intimately connected to the automobile boom and foreign investment. Although import substitution in general was slightly greater than during the previous period, import substitution became negative in four major sectors. The relative gain in substitution occurred in intermediate goods in-

[16]The Superintendency of Money and Credit issued Instruction 113 in early 1955. Under it, a foreign investor could import equipment by accepting payment in the form of a capital participation in the importing firm for favored industries.

[17]Both Baer in *Industrialization and Economic Development* and Furtado in *Diagnosis of the Brazilian Crisis* discuss these developments.

dustries. Domestic demand again began to rise in magnitude as the source of growth in consumer goods and investment and related goods while export demand fell in every sector.

Tentative Conclusions

The empirical analysis clears up several misconceptions regarding Brazil's industrialization. Furtado asserts that import substitution over the past three decades has been inseparable from the industrialization itself. In fact, this has been true only since 1953 (see Tables II and IV); substitution for imports prior to 1953 tended to be nominal, and was even negative in many SITC sectors. But neither is the converse statement by Baer accurate. Manufacturing products were not newly produced entirely inside Brazil in a very short time, for this had already been true with the exception of chemicals, paper, metals, and transport products by 1939 (see Table II).[18] The present analysis would also appear to vitiate the claim by Furtado that infant industry protection led to substitution in less essential products such as consumers' durables and luxuries rather than in heavy industry. The ISIC classification is somewhat misleading, however, for it includes consumer durables such as refrigerators, television sets, passenger autos, etc., as investment and related goods. Passenger autos became a particularly significant substitution item after 1958, and this finding raises problems of interpretation which are discussed in Part IV. The other durables, however, were insufficiently large and can be ignored. Thus, the sequential pattern of import substitution was not completely of the "classical" type;[19] although consumer goods, capital goods, and in-

---

[18]The Economic Commission for Latin America stresses the great degree of import substitution accomplished in all but the "very" capital intensive industries. However, evidence regarding the capital intensity of remaining industrial activities capable of substitution is unclear.

[19]Earlier import substitution processes for western countries are interestingly discussed in Alexander Gerschenkron, *Economic Backwardness in Historical Perspective* (Cambridge: Harvard University Press, 1962). Import substitution in Pakistan is discussed in Steve R. Lewis and Ronald Soligo, "Growth and Structural Change in Pakistan's Manufacturing Industry, 1954–1964," *Pakistan Development Review*, V, No. 1 (1965), 94–139. Cf. the Argentine case in Carlos Diaz Alejandro, *Exchange-Rate Devaluation in a Semi-Industrialized Country* (Cambridge: M.I.T. Press, 1966).

termediate goods, respectively, were substituted for imports, "durable" consumer goods became a major substitution item only during the final two periods.

The figures in Tables I, II, and IV point up the basic dissimilarities of sectoral expansion during the final two periods (1953–58 and 1959–63) . Sectoral growth and substitution were apportioned fairly evenly among all manufacturing sectors during the former period,

Table I

GROWTH RATES OF MANUFACTURING INDUSTRY
(Compounded Logarithmic)

ISIC No.	Industry Sector	1939–48	1948–53	1953–58	1959–63
Consumer Goods					
20–22	Food, beverages and tobacco	4.5	8.9	7.1	2.4
24	Clothing	4.6	5.1	9.3	0.9
25–26	Wood Products	13.7	6.6	2.8	0.8
28	Printing	3.6	10.5	7.5	3.7
29	Leather Products	1.3	2.4	5.4	0.3
Intermediate Goods					
23	Textiles	4.6	4.1	2.4	3.1
27	Paper	5.8	9.2	7.5	11.0
30	Rubber	21.3	14.5	5.7	1.1
31–32	Chemicals, petroleum and coal products	10.2	10.7	9.6	7.3
Investment and Related Goods					
33	Non-metallic minerals	11.9	12.7	4.4	1.2
34–38	Metals, machinery and equipment	13.5	4.1	13.9	21.0
Total	Manufacturing	11.6	6.3	8.0	9.0

Source: United Nations, *The Growth of World Industry,* National Tables 1938–61, Table 2B data for 1959–63 were calculated from IBGE/Conselho Nacional De Estatistica, *Anuario Estatistico Do Brasil, 1966* (Rio de Janeiro) , 130. ISIC Nos. 25–26, 31–32, and 34–38 were not listed in Table 2B, United Nations; these were calculated from value added data above and deflated by price indices from *International Financial Statistics,* wholesale prices excluding coffee; and *Conjunctura Economica,* sectoral price index series for years after 1944. Also see Appendix A.

Table II

PROPORTION OF DOMESTIC
PRODUCTION TO TOTAL SUPPLY (X÷Z)

Industry Sector	1938	1949	1953	1958	1963
Consumer goods	.9913	.9896	.9726	.9918	.9901
Intermediate goods	.8618	.8817	.8376	.8619	.9157
Investment and Related goods	.5701	.6666	.7223	.8218	.8931
Total	.8514	.8805	.8686	.8940	.9317

Source: See Appendix A; data source here is the same as for Table I.

Table III

PROPORTION OF EXPORTS
TO DOMESTIC PRODUCTION (E÷X)

Industry Sector	1938	1949	1953	1958	1963
Consumer Goods	.0092	.0096	.0106	.0209	.0128
Intermediate Goods	.0083	.0137	.0057	.0245	.0149
Investment and Related Goods	.0000	.0000	.0005	.0031	.0023
Total	.0049	.0092	.0071	.0168	.0100

Source: See Appendix A; data source here is the same as that for Table I.

whereas in the latter period, the converse occurred. This dichotomy (largely overlooked in the literature) is the primary clue to the roots of the post-1962 stagnation; it is examined more thoroughly in Part IV.

What do these results imply for future import substitution in Brazil? The data of Tables I–IV clearly demonstrate that import substitution had already been carried very far by 1939. Thus, continued across the board, import substitution between 1939 and 1963 was necessarily somewhat limited. That which did occur, however, absorbed to a large extent the remaining substitution possibilities. Over the next decade more than minor substitution could occur only in chemicals, petroleum, coal products, metals, machinery, and transport equipment (including durable consumer goods). Even in these sectors, "potential" future substitution is less than was "actual" substitution between 1953 and 1963 (Table II). An effort directed toward taking full advantage of this limited potential substitution is very questionable, for it would imply that a state of autarchy would be preferable to some trade. While international trade theory cannot demonstrate that "more" trade is better than "less" trade, it cannot be doubted that "some" trade is better than complete autarchy. Since Brazil already has one of the lowest import coefficients in the world, efforts to increase trade along appropriate lines will likely bring greater benefits than will a further diminution of trade. The argument of the next section goes even further: that substitution for imports has already gone too far in some industrial sectors in terms of (high) opportunity cost.

Table IV
SOURCES OF GROWTH

Industrial Sector	1949–53			1953–58			1958–63		
	Domestic Demand	Exports	Import Substitution	Domestic Demand	Exports	Import Substitution	Domestic Demand	Exports	Import Substitution
Consumer goods	1.0232	.0115	−.0350	.9417	.0270	.0311	.9902	.0117	−.0019
Intermediate goods	1.1057	−.0018	−.1041	.9311	.0270	.0400	.9227	.0119	.0654
Investment and Related goods	.8666	.0006	.1328	.8429	.0028	.1544	.9105	.0018	.0877
Total	1.0220	.0045	−.0265	.9403	.0185	.0413	.9467	.0082	.0447

Source: See Appendix A for definitions. For source of calculations see Donald Huddle, "Notes on the Brazilian Industrialization: Sources of Growth and Structural Change," Center Discussion Paper No. 30 (Yale University, June, 1967).

A Tentative Interpretation

This section attempts to provide a stylized synthesis of the Brazilian industrialization. Previous authors have emphasized the key roles played by inflation, exchange control, inter-industry linkages, and the terms of trade. Their assessment of the process by which these variables operated on the economy, however, has not always been clear and accurate. Previous studies have differed also in their assessment of the success of the industrialization. For instance, industrial growth has been characterized as both balanced (Baer) and unbalanced (Furtado) ; choices made by the government have been evaluated as good, though relatively unplanned (Baer) , and as poor (Furtado) , etc. In what follows, these and other aspects of the industrialization are analyzed.

During the early postwar years the government greatly influenced the course of events but much less comprehensively and successfully than after 1953. Only after the exchange control system was drastically improved in October, 1953, and large-scale financing of industrial activities commenced did the manufacturing sector begin its high growth phase. Table V illustrates the power which the government exercised after 1953 on the private sectors. The placement of an import in either the favored or the penalty category determined the viability of all import-competing domestic activities. Favored sectors could import capital and intermediate goods at one-fifth to one-sixth the exchange cost of other sectors. The former also received absolute protection from foreign competitors. A second major weapon of the authorities was control of finance capital. Loans of the monetary authorities and the National Development Bank rose continuously in real terms, and up to 1959 were equivalent in amount to "total" private fixed capital investment in industry. Other sources of funds for long-term investments were comparatively insignificant. Commercial banks typically loaned short-term and the capital market was too underdeveloped to provide funds on any scale. Retained earnings, on the other hand, were fairly small until 1959. Finally, the government became an increasingly important direct investor. By 1962 new government fixed investment surpassed that of the private sector. In the last two columns of Table VI are shown the noninflationary sources of government expenditure.

Two facts are prominent in the context of industrial growth and import substitution in Brazil. First, between 1953 and 1958 both the rate of growth and import substitution as a source of growth were high and reasonably well apportioned among all manufacturing sectors (see Tables I and IV). Second, after 1958 this balance was lost and rapid growth and substitution were confined to several industries—metals, machinery and transport equipment, and chemicals and paper industries (see Table I). These facts tend to contradict the notion that the impetus of industrialization was lost as soon as the external terms of trade turned against Brazil in 1954 (Furtado), or only when social imbalances and political uncertainties arose in the early 1960's (Baer). Only after 1958 did there arise excess capacity in some sectors (textiles, household appliances, transport materials, and light equipment) and under capacity in others (basic metallurgical, chemicals, rubber, and paper).[20]

In my opinion, these developments were not primarily a consequence of either reduced price-wage lags or the worsening external terms of trade. Price-wage lags per se have never been demonstrably important. The data do not reveal a price-wage lag. Though Baer argues that sizable transfers could have occurred since taxes were regressive and rising, this hypothesis cannot be tested;[21] data on tax incidence and regressivity are unavailable. However, in Appendix B, an indirect test of the hypothesis shows that the data are inconsistent with the notion that regressivity led to transfers which significantly raised the saving rate. Given that the savings coefficient did not increase in Brazil despite rapidly rising income, either the redistribution effect was small or entrepreneurs' marginal savings rates were little higher than the wage and salary earners'; or alternatively other unidentified factors reduced transfers/savings. One decisive point is undisputed—the government financed industry in an amount equivalent to total fixed capital formation in industry

[20]Cf. United Nations, "The Growth and Decline of Import Substitution in Brazil," 52.
[21]Cf. Baer, *Industrialization and Economic Development in Brazil.*

between 1953 and 1958 (Table V) . Although industry's use of these funds is indeterminant, it is clear that they constituted an important source of subsidized financing alternative to saving out of current profits. Firms financed so generously may well have reduced saving out of profits, which would help explain the absence of a rising saving coefficient for the economy.[22]

A stylized interpretation of the rise and fall of industrialization in Brazil, which is consistent with the findings presented above is the following: the manufacturing sector responded strongly to the various government incentives which greatly raised the marginal efficiency of investment. The inflation essentially operated so as to transfer resources from other sectors of the economy to the government; in turn the government lent these resources to favored industrial sectors. Although price-wage lags per se were unimportant, domestic infant industries profitably expanded. These firms—oligopolists and monopolists with a protected domestic market—received government loan subsidies which *averaged* from 20 to 30 percent of *total* industrial profits (to the favored industries much more.) [23]

Only by the late 1950's did unfavorable factors appear. The first of these was the phenomenon of rising costs in the subsidized sectors. As the industrialization widened, the original infant industries had to purchase more and more inputs from new high cost infants. These later protected infants were often unreliable in meeting quotas, deadlines, and specifications.[24] The older industries tried to offset the threat to their price-cost structures through vertical in-

[22]The savings coefficient actually fell slightly between 1947–48 and 1957–58, and then increased by 1962–63. Overall, there was no apparent upward trend. Source: *Revista Brasileira de Economia,* Fundacao Getulio Vargas.

[23]Loan subsidies were calculated by assuming that the market interest rate would have exceeded the observed rate of price increase (implicit deflator) by 12 percent. The actual interest rate of the National Bank for Economic Development and the monetary authorities which varied from 10 to 14 percent was substracted from the assumed market rate and the resulting figure was multiplied by total loans to get the subsidy figure. Subsidies were cr. 2.45 bil. in 1953 and cr. 7164 bil. in 1958. Imputed industry profits were cr. .9 bil. in 1953 and cr. 38.9 bil. in 1958.

[24]Cf. Lincoln Gordon and Engelbert L. Grommers, *United States Manufacturing Investment in Brazil* (Cambridge: Harvard School of Business, 1962) , which discusses many difficulties of U.S. firms in obtaining inputs in terms of price, quality, and delivery dates.

tegration, but this was a pallative for the firm and not the economy. Second, incomes began to be redirected to the formerly neglected, penalized sectors (agriculture and wage earners). This redistribution operated partly through normal market forces. For instance, productivity in the primary sector tended to suffer as a consequence of its relative unprofitability. As production lagged, and could not be offset by larger imports, primary product prices began to rise. Also, as prices of wage goods began to rise, workers were able to demand and receive higher wages. The interplay of these forces— urbanization, rising incomes, and only slowly increasing productivity in the primary sector—greatly reduced the amount of resources which could be transferred to industry. By 1958, government transfers to industry were increasingly offset by the intersectoral shift in the terms of trade.[25] Efforts to neutralize this development through price controls and export restrictions on primary products were unsuccessful.[26] Instead, these measures mainly reduced the capacity to import and drove up the exchange price of imports.[27]

Partly because of the above circumstances, the government shifted its efforts toward large-scale substitution in the automotive sector. Through numerous inducements, foreign and domestic investors increased the domestic coefficient of total supply of motor vehicles from about .42 in 1958 to .98 in 1963. [28] These coefficients overstate the extent of import substitution, however. Imports of accessories increased in value roughly in proportion to motor vehicle production; moreover, (backward linked) supplying industries, e.g., iron and steel, machines and equipment, rubber, etc., required higher

[25]The terms of trade between agriculture and industry were almost constant between 1948 and 1954. They began to rise slightly in favor of agriculture up to 1958 and then turned precipitously against industry (117 to 138 between the years 1958 and 1962 from an index of 100 in 1953). Source: *Plano Trienal,* Presidencia Da Republica, (Rio de Janeiro ,1963) and *Conjunctura Economica* (May, 1965).

[26]Cf. M. S. Simonsen, *Os Controles de Precos na Economia Brasileira,* (Rio de Janeiro: CONSULTEC, 1961).

[27]Restrictions could be used to prevent the export of any primary commodity deemed to be in short supply domestically. Outright prohibitions were not common, but the possibility of prohibition probably constituted an important disincentive to development of foreign markets.

[28]Calculated from value data in Gordon and Grommers, *United States Manufacturing in Brazil,* 63; and IBGE, *Anuario Estatistico* (Rio de Janeiro) , various dates.

imports in order to meet automotive demand. It is likely that the massive push in motor vehicles entailed high (net) social costs. Government switching of financial and foreign exchange resources from the more traditional and early infants to motor vehicles and related industries caught the former sectors in a debilitating squeeze which was accentuated after 1957 by the worsening domestic terms of trade (see Table IV and 31 n.) . The much greater availability of passenger autos after 1958 (comprising about half of vehicle production)[29] diminished domestic demand for products of industries unlinked to the newly favored industries. Since many of these unfavored sectors already had excess capacity, reduced demand for their products resulted in lower growth rates. In terms of both consumption and foreign exchange use, the wisdom of making available and subsidizing passenger autos in partial substitution for the products of the neglected sectors seems questionable.[30] Finally, the substitution for imports of domestically produced tractors and other primary sector inputs partly, or wholly, offset reductions in cost and the productivity of subsidies to the agricultural sector.[31] On these considerations, therefore, cost-push inflation and dualism were aggravated.

In retrospect, the new industrialization strategy in 1957–58 had high opportunity costs. If policy had been focused instead on removing disincentives in the agricultural and export sectors, while retaining the incentives earlier given to a broad spectrum of manufacturing industries, the post-1962 stagnation, as well as increasing unemployment and under-employment, might have been averted. The industrialization had many anti-employment biases, some of which were natural, given the greater productivity of capital-intensive techniques in many lines. The fact that substitution and rapid expansion were centered in capital and intermediate goods after 1952 also meant that the industrialization would be skewed toward capital-intensive factor proportions. But capital intensive

[29]Calculated from Gordon and Grommers, United States Manufacturing, 63.

[30]The concepts of social essentiality is rather subjective, but I would expect passenger autos to be less essential to the population at large than food, clothing, and housing. Government subsidies to the former would be difficult to justify.

[31]Apparently, fewer tractors were available after the large-scale substitution than even a decade earlier. IBGE, *Anuario Estatistico,* various issues.

Table V
INDICATORS OF GOVERNMENT INFLUENCE ON INDUSTRY

	Exchange Rates For: (cruzeiros per U.S. dollar)		Loans to Industry by: (billions of 1949 cruzeiros)			Private Industry's (billions of 1949 cruzeiros)			Government's: (billions of 1949 cruzeiros)	
	(1)* Favored Imports	(2) Penalty Imports	(3) Total Imports	(4) Monetary Authorities	(5) BNDE	(6) Fixed Investment	(7) Retained Earnings	(8) Fixed Investment	(9) Fixed Exchange Revenue	(10) Other Revenue
1953	40	195	49	10	.8	12.	5.5	9.1		41.7
1954	55	200	62	12.3	.8	13.	7.3	10.4	3.0	47.7
1955	55	340	114	12.3	.8	11.	7.3	9.6	– .1	46.0
1956	70	320	112	12.2	.8	13.	6.7	9.2	3.7	47.2
1957	70	310	88	13.5	.6	14.	6.4	14.5	4.4	51.6
1958	80	360	152	14.5	1.5	16.	9.6	18.1	4.0	62.7
1959	120	320	203	13.3	.9	18.	14.0	17.6	.7	68.3
1960	120	450	228	13.2	1.9	23.	20.2	20.7	10.5	81.4
1961	120	620	240	14.0	.9	21.		20.7		73.1
1962				16.6	.3	20.		25.5		70.0

* (1) "Cost of exchange" plus official rate as of Aug. 1, of each year.

(2) Category V plus official rate as of Aug. 1, between 1953 and 1957; special category rate plus official rate between 1958 and 1961.

(3) Weighted average exchange rate plus official rate. Tariffs became important after 1957 but are not included because of data unavailability.

(4) to (10) in 1949 prices; G.N.P. deflator.

(6) Sectoral investment data are not available for Brazil. Therefore from total gross fixed investment, industrial gross fixed investment had to be estimated by assuming that its incremental capital output ratio was 50 percent higher than the ICOR for the entire economy. This assumption is consistent with industrial ICOR's found in other industrializing economies. However, the estimates are crude and intended for illustration of the trend.

(7) Retained earnings in industry were estimated by deducting the commercial sector's share of total retained earnings by its weighted share of product.

(9) Net of exchange earnings used to purchase coffee.

Source: Columns (1)–(3), Banco de Brasil; (4), (5) & (9), calculated from *Boletim Superintendencia de Moedas e Credito* (July, 1966); (6), (7), (8), and (10), *Revista Brasileira de Economia, Fundação Getúlio Vargas* (March, 1962 and 1967).

factor use was unnecessarily encouraged in two ways: (1) import subsidies excluded labor (a non-traded good internationally) and were not offset by domestic subsidies for labor use; (2) sectors favored by the government, especially after 1957–58, tended to have higher capital/labor ratios than other manufacturing industries, though not noticeably higher productivity. Although the anti-employment biases of these developments might have been offset if the production and incomes created had caused a heightened demand for high productivity services and primary products, the contrary seems to have occurred. While labor force growth in services more than doubled that of industry, productivity in the former sector actually declined between 1950–60; agricultural workers fared little better.[32] The data (admittedly incomplete) indicate that the factor share of labor fell over time; and along with it the distribution of income probably became more unequal.[33] In welfare terms, these findings imply that the fruits of rapid GNP growth and industrialization in the Brazilian instance may well have bypassed the unskilled, working-age masses. It is particularly in this sense that the economic events of the postwar years in Brazil have been so disappointing.

Conclusions

The empirical findings of this paper have dispelled some of the inaccurate and contradictory notions of the sources and patterns of Brazilian industrialization. However, it has been necessary to go beyond what can be accurately ascertained. Any reasonably com-

[32]Labor force growth was slightly higher than product growth in service (5.2 percent p.a. versus 5.1 percent p.a.) between 1950 and 1960. Source: census data.

Labor productivity increased in agriculture (at about 2 percent p.a. between 1950 and 1960), but it is well known that agricultural labor still receives far less than the minimum wage in most areas. The minimum wage multiplied by the number of workers in the sector exceeds the total product by a wide margin. The plight of wage labor in rural regions is well drawn in Furtado, *Diagnosis of the Brazilian Crisis;* and Robert Alexander, *Labor Relations in Argentina, Brazil, and Chile* (New York: McGraw-Hill, Inc., 1962).

[33]Both the wage share in total value added (industry) and the ratio of workers remuneration to total profits began to fall during the 1950's after having risen in the late 1940's. Source: Data from Fundaco Gétulio Vargas, "Contas Nacionais do Brasil," *Revista Brasileira de Economia* (March, 1962).

plete evaluation and interpretation of the import-substitution industrialization in Brazil must be somewhat speculative and intuitive, for there are as yet no means available for accessing completely the incentives and disincentives provided by the government. Nor can either the size of intersectoral transfers or the long-run dynamic comparative advantage of the industries artificially created be measured.

Although only reliable and extensive data will clarify many specific issues, the necessary condition for increased long-run social welfare in Brazil will most probably be radical reform in the primary sector, not the least of which would be the rationalization of coffee production and pricing rather than heavily subsidized import-substitution industrialization. The present government is apparently aware of the many complex problems which it faces—growing unemployment and under-employment especially in the urban centers for unskilled labor,[34] inequitable income distribution, a stagnant export sector, and low productivity agriculture. Whether it will have the political courage and means with which to implement the basic reforms which will necessarily be unpopular with powerful landed and industrial oligarchs is another question. Up to now, the increased welfare of *o povo* has been only an incidental by-product of the industrialization. To remedy both the poverty and the fragmented nature of the economy, however, may well require measures which are innovative and revolutionary. As of early 1968 the Costa e Silva government's policies offer little cause for optimism. Some measure of economic growth and recovery from the recent stagnation are to be expected, but the critical, longer-run problems of social and economic development have yet not been faced up to by the government.

[34]Population migration into the south-central regions has been estimated at over 5 percent annually for the 1950–60 decade. Industrial labor growth has been only 2.5 percent annually during the same period despite a product growth of almost 9 percent annually. Source: calculated from census data 1950 and 1960.

Most of the migrants have found employment in petty services. Employment growth in services was 5.2 percent annually between 1950 and 1960 although real product growth in the services sector was only about 5 percent. The inactive to working-age population ratio rose during the period. Source: calculated from census data 1950 and 1960.

Appendix A

Growth sources of manufacturing industry were apportioned among domestic demand, [A], export demand, [B], and import substitution, [C], according to the following equation:

$$
\text{(1)} \quad \triangle X = \underbrace{\left[\frac{X_1}{Z_1} \cdot \triangle (D+W) \right]}_{[A]} + \underbrace{\left[\frac{X_1}{Z_1} \cdot \triangle E \right]}_{[B]} + \underbrace{\left[\left(\frac{X_2}{Z_2} - \frac{X_1}{Z_1} \right) \cdot Z_2 \right]}_{[C]}
$$

Where X is defined as domestic production, Z as total supply, D as domestic demand, W as domestic intermediate demand, and E as foreign demand for exports, and the subscripts refer to the beginning and ending points in time.

The contribution of domestic demand and export demand is calculated by assuming that the proportion of domestic production to total supply did not change during the period. Import substitution (liberalization) is then calculated as the change in the proportion of domestic production to total supply during the period times the most recent total supply.

The identity equations on which equation (1) is based are explained in Huddle, "Notes on the Brazilian Industrialization: Sources of Growth and Structural Change," Center Discussion Paper No. 30 (Yale University, June, 1967). For further references to equation (1) also see: Stephen R. Lewis and Ronald Soligo, "Growth and Structural Change in Pakistan's Manufacturing Industry, 1954–1964," *The Pakistan Development Review*, V (Spring, 1965), 94–139; and Som Liem "Sources and Direction of Growth In Manufacturing Industries: Argentina, Brazil, and Chile (1938–1958)," mimeographed. Brazilian data sources and procedures of estimation are discussed in the latter. However, a caveat should be mentioned here which applies to this as well as other quantitative studies of industrialization in regard to the unreliability and coverage of data on manufacturing industry. Coverage is limited first to firms of five or more employees. Thus, even during a census year significant amounts of production are excluded from measured output. Moreover, except during census years (every decade in Brazil) data on industrial production is derived from only a sample of firms (8,060 of 40,790 total estimated in the year 1963). The reliability of the data for even the covered firms is open to serious question. However, since alternative means of estimation do not exist, the data must be used, although not without attaching to the results an error coefficient perhaps as high as ± 25 percent. The best available general discussion of Brazilian income and product statistics is found in Werner Baer, *Industrialization and Economic Development in Brazil* (Homewood, Ill.: Richard D. Irwin, 1965), Appendix A.

Appendix B
Redistribution Effects of Inflation in Brazil

To test the frequently postulated assertion that *post-tax* income was redistributed from consuming to entrepreneurial classes in Brazil, a simple model is developed here which relates an increase in direct taxes with an increase in saving. Let

(1) $S_t = S_c + S_e$

where S_t is total saving, S_e is entrepreneurial saving, and S_c is consumer saving.

(2) $S_c = (1\text{-}a) \quad (cY\text{-}dTi)$

where for the consuming classes after tax saving is determined by a (the average propensity to consume), c (the proportion of GNP which it receives) and d (the proportion of indirect tax, Ti).

(3) $S_e = (1\text{-}b) \ [(1\text{-}c) \ Y] + dTi$

where for the entrepreneurial class, b is the average propensity to consume and dTi is assumed to be completely saved by the government. Therefore

(4) $S_t = (1\text{-}a) \quad (cY\text{-}dTi) + (1\text{-}b) \ [(1\text{-}c) \ Y] + dTi$

Values for the variables based on Brazilian data are inserted as follows: a = .9, b = .7, c = .7, and Y = 100. Y is chosen for convenience. c was the actual share of consumer classes. Values for a and b were derived from a set of simultaneous equations which would yield a propensity to save for the consuming class one-third of that of the entrepreneurial class to approximate Hendrik S. Houthakker's findings. These values were also designed to yield the rate of saving achieved by Brazil. Two values were selected for d, one which would place the indirect tax burden equally among the saving and consuming classes (.50) and one (.67) which would reflect regressive incidence. The beginning year value of Ti was 10 and the end value 15, both of which correspond to indirect taxes in the years 1950 and 1960.

The results are rather surprising. The 50 percent increase in indirect taxes leads to an increase in total saving as a percentage of GNP of only 3 percent if d = .67 and only 2.25 percent if d = .5.

Thus, even for these relatively favorable values for the variables, the increase in saving is small, and would be smaller still if the acknowledged *pre-tax* income shift over these years to wage earners had been included.

Therefore, despite the numerous assertions that wage lags and regressive indirect taxes did occur, it is most significant that neither marginal nor total savings rose in Brazil during the postwar years. Indirectly, these findings support the hypothesis that entrepreneurial classes had a not much higher propensity to save than did the consuming classes.

Education and Modernization in Brazil

John V. D. Saunders

THE RELATIONSHIP OF EDUCATION TO SOCIAL CHANGE IN GENERAL AND to that particular kind of social change which we are here calling modernization is uncontested.[1] Education may foster modernization through the creation of a population more willing to accept technical innovations and make use of them: by diffusing among the population the skills, organizational, administrative, and technical, which are necessary for the institution of changes and for the inevitable accommodation to these same changes; and by instilling in students, through the classroom and school situation, aspirations beyond their present means to achieve while, at the same time, equipping them with the means with which to achieve them. By creating thus, that necessary dissatisfaction with the personal status quo of a significant number of individuals without which the motivation to innovate and effect changes would be in short supply in the society.

[1]Grateful acknowledgment is made to the U.S. Office of Education for a faculty research grant which made possible the research on which this paper is based. I am especially indebted for materials in the first section to an unpublished paper by Anisio Teixeira entitled "A Educação e a Sociedade Brasileira." Also: Robert J. Havighurst and J. Roberto Moreira, *Society and Education in Brazil* (Pittsburgh: University of Pittsburgh Press, 1965), 54–59, 71–76; Maria José Garcia Werebe, *Grandezas e Misérias do Ensino Brasileiro* (São Paulo: Difusão Européia do Livro, 1963), *passim*.

The Evolution of Education in Brazil

The Portuguese colonial regime in Brazil placed severe limitations on the activities permitted the colonists. The prohibition of printing presses and higher education along with censorship exercised over the importation of printed matter were allied with restrictions of an economic and political nature designed to preserve Portuguese dominance over all phases of the life of the colony.

Basic education was provided by schools established by religious orders, notably the Jesuits; by institutions of more advanced learning in Portugal and France; and by the arrival of the Portuguese born and reared who had acquired their education in the Mother Country. The basic educational needs of the clergy and of the colonial administration were met in the context of a highly stratified colonial society. Education served, basically, the function of providing the personnel essential to the maintenance of an unenviable colonial status.

After the expulsion of the Jesuits in 1759, this situation was modified by the establishment of schools by the Crown. Education remained, however, the privilege of a small ruling class and functioned to preserve the existing social order.

The advent of independence and the establishment of the monarchy in the nineteenth century witnessed an important structural change in educational policy although its functions remained essentially the same. The provinces, to be called states after the establishment of the Republic, were entrusted with "popular" education at the primary and *vocational* secondary levels. The privileged status of the upper class with regard to access to higher education was preserved by denying admission to the universities to the graduates of these schools. This function was retained by the handful of *academic* secondary schools which were highly selective in their admission policies. Credits were not transferable from vocational to academic secondary schools. Thus the Crown, which had gained control over education during the colonial period with the reforms instituted by the Marquis of Pombal and the expulsion of the Jesuits, used its new powers to control access to higher education, in effect limiting it to the elite, while providing a second-class education on a small scale to other segments of freemen in the society.

The educational norms and practices followed during the Empire produced a dual educational system. One oriented toward the so-called popular masses and the provision of minimal educational and artisanship skills for that segment of society, and another oriented toward the training of an elite whose major function was the maintenance of the existing social order and the preparation of individuals to assume the higher ranking positions in the social structure and administrative hierarchy. Education became, in essence, the characteristic which conferred upon those who possessed it special privileges and status. It was a system appropriate to a static society in which very little change occurred and none was contemplated. Some indication of the static nature of Brazilian society during the Monarchy and early Republican period is provided by the fact that real per capita income did not increase between 1872 and 1900. [2]

The Republican government did little to change this situation. Public funds supported but one academic secondary school, the Colégio Dom Pedro II in Rio, used as a model institution that set standards for other secondary schools which gained what amounted to accreditation by demonstrating equivalency to the model institution. Private accredited secondary schools were maintained in the capitals of the most important states. Graduation from an academic secondary school was a prerequisite for admission to institutions of higher learning. Higher education was, therefore, restricted almost exclusively to the elite. State supported primary and vocational secondary schools did not grant access to higher education and so did not represent a threat to the privileged status of the upper classes. The emphasis in academic secondary schools was on an encyclopaedic curriculum weighted toward the rote learning of traditional humanistic subjects. Their curricula were almost entirely devoid of subject matter which represented any change in the basic concepts and orientation of the educational system.

[2]Havighurst and Moreira, *Society and Education in Brazil*, 98.

Beginning especially in the 1920's, although the roots of this trend date from the middle of the nineteenth century, the state supported educational systems were captured by a developing middle class. The normal school, intended as a vocational secondary school to prepare girls as primary teachers, had long since become a prestigeful training ground for the daughters of middle-class families. Primary schools at first intended to provide a minimum educational foundation for the masses became transformed by the social and hence educational aspirations of the middle class into selective schools whose unstated aim was the preparation of the student for the admission exams into academic secondary institutions and, eventually, institutions of higher learning.

Middle-class aspirations created enormous pressures for the expansion of academic secondary education. These pressures were met by the proliferation of private institutions, the bulk of which were run as profit-making enterprises, offering, at a price the new middle class could afford to pay, academic instruction preparatory for university entrance examinations. The consequent balooning of secondary enrollments is documented elsewhere in these pages.

The dual nature of the Brazilian educational system was somewhat analogous to the English system in which, at the conclusion of primary school, students are selected who are considered worthy of an academic secondary education, which can lead to a university education. The remaining students are relegated to secondary modern schools largely vocational in their orientation. In England, however, this selection is accomplished by means of examination at age eleven—the notorious elevenses—on termination of the primary curriculum, while in Brazil the selection was assured by an implicit socioeconomic discrimination.

As the nation developed during the period following the First World War and large numbers came to acquire the aspirations concomitant with an academic secondary education and the economic means with which to achieve them, the pressure for what amounted to a democratization, Brazilian style, of the educational system eroded the barriers between the two educational systems, so that secondary education granting access to higher learning became the universal norm, and the special status of the graduates of academic secondary schools disappeared. Secondary education, to be sure, is still largely private, but to the considerable extent that these institutions have expanded and multiplied and to which a significant segment of the population has acquired the means with which to afford it, educational opportunity and the accessibility of secondary education has been greatly broadened. This broadening was not achieved, however, without the payment of a price. The encyclopaedic curricula of the Ginásio and Colégio, the first (four-year) and second (three-year) cycles of secondary education, respectively, which included a total of seventeen subjects during the seven-year course of study, made demands on the available supply of qualified teachers that could not be met. Thus, in spite of federal inspection intended to assure conformity to academic standards for which the Colégio Dom Pedro II served as a national model, many academic secondary institutions were largely makeshift both with regard to physical facilities and instructional personnel. "The final result obtained was highly paradoxical. Because the nation fought for an intellectual education for its dominant classes, this type of education became the most prestigeful and the most desired, experiencing a disorderly expansion and, with the expansion, losing its possible characteristics. The improvisation resulting from this rapid growth led other branches of secondary education to demand and obtain equivalence of their courses to the academic curriculum so that they also might grant access to higher learning, making them as well preparatory for institutions of higher learning." [3]

Thus, in the 1950's, the entire educational system had become oriented toward admission to the halls of higher learning and eventual acquisition of the social patents which would give access to the privileges of the elite. The number that attained this goal is in good measure controlled by largely arbitrary devices. The drop-out rate at all levels is high. Those students who complete primary school face an admission examination for entrance into secondary school, and if successful in the completion of secondary school require-

[3] Teixeira, "A Educação e a Sociedade Brasileira."

ments, they then face the dreaded vestibular or university entrance examinations.

In spite of the rapid reduction of the student population as it progresses from year to year through the educational system, the large increase in the number of students completing their secondary education has created new pressures, during the last decade, on institutions of higher learning, pressures similar to those exerted in the 1930's on secondary education. The response has been the establishment of a considerable number of new public, state, and sometimes municipally supported colleges, frequently in the smaller cities of the several states. Usually the college begins with a faculty of philosophy, science, and letters—less expensive to establish and equip and easier to staff than other faculties—which is similar in its curriculum to a college of arts and sciences, and eventually may expand to include other faculties. Although much the same criticism can be made of many of these institutions as were made of the expanding private academic secondary schools, they hold the advantage, for the first time in the history of Brazil, of moving higher education from the handful of large and politically important cities into geographic locations of greater accessibility to the bulk of the population.

The balance of this paper will be devoted to a consideration of three basic characteristics of the educational system of Brazil: availability or accessibility of education to the population; promotion within the educational system; and training in modern as well as traditional professional subjects or specialties at secondary and especially higher levels of instruction. In addition to these characteristics which are more or less amenable to statistical analysis, the more intangible question of whether or not the school contributes to the development of personality types which promote rather than resist modernization will be explored in what must be a speculative fashion.

General Educational Trends

The twenty-year period from 1940 to 1960 was one of intense

social change in Brazilian society. Among the notable changes which occurred was a substantial increase in the literacy of the Brazilian population, reflecting principally an increase in primary enrollments.

Although literacy made substantial gains between 1940 and 1950, the most spectacular increases occurred between 1950 and 1960 (Figure 1). Gains occurred at all age levels, but most notably in the ten to twenty age group, as primary education gained momentum, and ever increasing numbers and percentages of Brazilians were able to receive at least the minimal skills of reading and writing by primary school attendance. In 1960 two-thirds of the population in the fifteen to thirty age bracket were able to read and write, so that the literacy of that portion of the population upon which much of

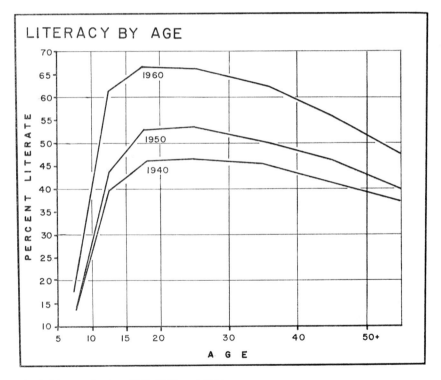

Fig. 1—Literacy by Age, 1940, 1950, and 1960.

the thrust for modernization depends is rising consistently and rapidly. Of even greater significance are increases in male literacy, especially among persons in the productive ages of fifteen to forty (Figure 2). Between 1940 and 1960, the proportion of males fifteen to twenty years old who read and write increased from 46 to 66 percent and that of males in the twenty to thirty age group from 52 to 69 percent.

Although primary school enrollments and literacy have taken notable strides since 1940, it is the upward pressure on secondary education by the increasingly large and prosperous middle class that resulted in the most spectacular enrollment trends. These same pressures have been felt at the higher levels of education as well and have produced a comparable but less intense expansion of enroll-

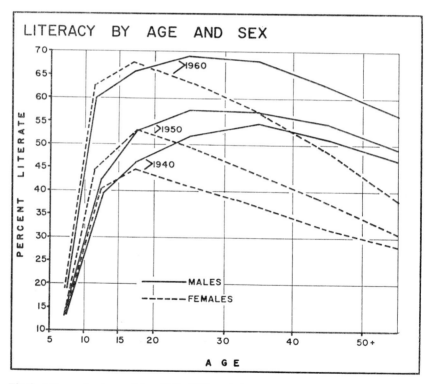

Fig. 2—Literacy by Age and Sex, 1940, 1950, and 1960.

ments in higher education (Figure 3). This expansion has occurred partly as a result of increased primary enrollments but principally by a lowered drop-out rate, so that ever increasing numbers of children, proportionately, who enter the first grade survive to more advanced grade levels than previously, before dropping out. Thus, while survival rates are still exceedingly low, of 1,000 students entering first grade in 1942 only 155 survived to the fourth grade, while

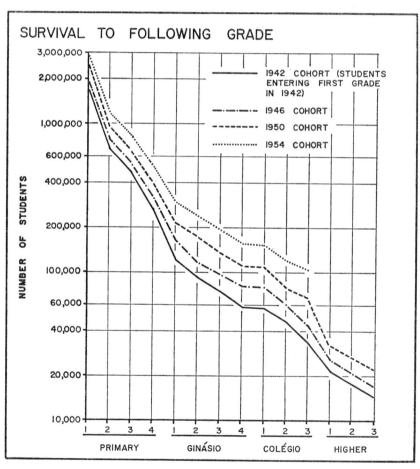

Fig. 3—Numbers of Students Attaining Stated Levels of Enrollment, 1942, 1946, 1950, and 1954 Cohorts.

in 1953 the comparable figure was 180, an increase of 16 percent
(Table 1). Survival rates for the last year of the Ginásio, the first
secondary cycle, and for the last year of the Colégio, the second
secondary cycle, increased by 43 and 70 percent, respectively, during
the same period. Increasing proportions of primary school graduates
are seeking admission to secondary schools after completing their
secondary education.

Table 1

NUMBER OF STUDENTS ATTAINING STATED
LEVELS OF ENROLLMENT PER THOUSAND
ENROLLING IN THE FIRST GRADE IN
1942, 1947, AND 1953

Enrollment Level	COHORT		
	1942	1947	1953
Last Year Primary	155	172	180
First Year Ginásio	71	81	98
Last Year Ginásio	35	43	51
First Year Colégio	34	43	50
Last Year Colégio	20	27	34
First Year University	13	14	17
Third Year University	9	9	—

Enrollments at all educational levels have been increasing during
the three decades or so since 1932 (Figure 4). The sharpest rates of
increase have occurred in secondary and higher education. Urban
primary enrollments have increased more rapidly than rural primary enrollments, reflecting the greater proportionate investment
in urban than in rural education, as well as the more rapid population increase of urban places. Academic as opposed to vocational
secondary education has not only had greater numbers enrolled
but has increased more rapidly, since it has traditionally been more
prestigeful and has allowed access to higher education. The skills
and training received at the secondary level are prerequisites to the
development of the myriad of technical, secretarial, industrial, com-

mercial, and other skills upon which a modernized society depends
for the performance of services essential to the functioning of the

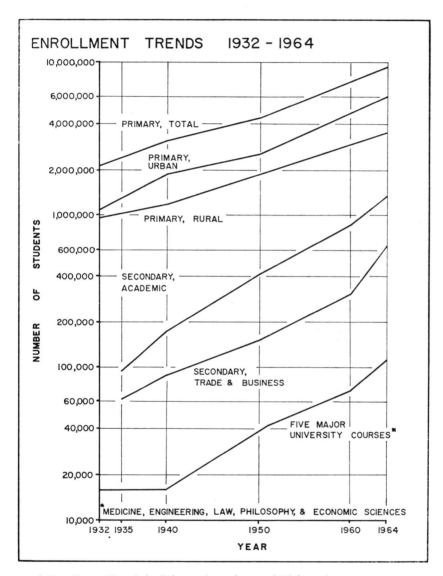

Fig. 4—Enrollment Trends for Primary, Secondary, and Higher Education, 1932–64.

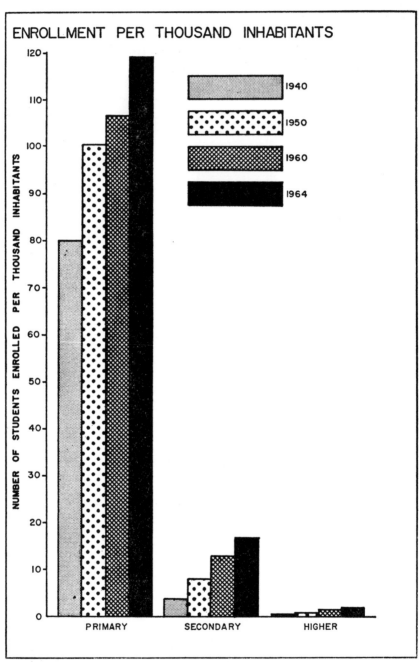

Fig. 5—Enrollment in Primary, Secondary, and Higher Education, Per Thousand Inhabitants, 1940, 1950, 1960, and 1964.

overall structure. Also, these skills contribute to social differentia-
tion and the development of an intermediate group—not to say
middle class—between the dominant upper classes and the mal-
educated masses.

Although secondary and higher education has expanded more
rapidly than elementary education, the gap between them in terms
of comparative enrollment figures is still enormous. In 1964 there
were 119 elementary students enrolled per thousand population.
This figure dropped, however, to 17 for secondary school students
and plunged to 1.8 for those pursuing courses of higher learning
(Figure 5). To achieve secondary enrollment levels comparable to
those of North America and Western Europe, Brazil will have to
expand secondary enrollments four or five times in addition to the
added expansion necessitated by a rapidly increasing school age
population.

The prospects for such an expansion, along with its implications
for the modernization of the society, are better than one might expect. Since the 1930's, at least, secondary enrollment has increased
at a rate well in excess of that of the population. This trend was especially accentuated from 1950 to 1964. During those years secondary enrollment skyrocketed by 251 percent while the population grew by 54 percent. Furthermore as secondary education grows,
so does the middle class, its prime beneficiary and principal source
of support—in turn creating a further demand and resource base
producing a rapid cumulative effect. One reason why this cumulative effect is possible is that secondary education, as opposed to primary education, is largely private and, therefore, directly dependent
for financial support on that portion of the population that is most
willing and able to contribute to its maintenance and has the most
to gain by so doing. This situation has tended to change but little
over the years. In 1929, private schools enrolled 89 percent of secondary students and in 1962, 61 percent. During the same period,
the proportion of primary students enrolled in private schools was
nearly halved, dropping from 20 to 12 percent. Thus the nation has,
in effect, depended on the comparatively affluent classes to finance
much of secondary education out of their own pockets while con-

centrating public funds at the primary and higher educational levels.

Nevertheless, it is evident that this situation presents a severe limitation with regard to accessibility. In effect, secondary education is generally available only to those who can afford to pay the cost of privately supported instruction, while large numbers of students from the economically less advantaged classes compete among themselves, and with children from middle-class homes as well, for the limited number of seats in the public secondary schools. As the society modernizes, this limitation of accessibility to secondary education will need to be reduced for the process to continue at an even pace.

That this is occurring in Brazil seems to be indicated by the fact that in Brazil's most developed region, the South, the proportion of secondary students enrolled in public schools is the greatest, presenting a sharp contrast with the remaining regions of the nations in this respect. Likewise, not surprisingly, there is a sharp difference between educational expenditures per capita between the South and other regions (Figure 6). The state of Sao Paulo, the major component of this region, not only has a per capita expenditure which is nearly two and one-half times larger than the national average, but also budgets 44 percent of the total state funds spent for education in Brazil. The South as a whole spends 59 percent of such funds. There is, indeed, a myriad of indices that reflect not only the greater modernization of the South, but also an increasing differential especially between it and the North and Northeast regions of the nation. To the extent that the latter are problem areas because of these differentials rather than because of their actual levels of development, those areas will tend to become more rather than less problematic with the passage of time as a result of the increase of these differentials.

PRIMARY EDUCATION

The question of accessibility to primary education has been largely solved in Brazil. Some distortions remain and will probably

not be eliminated for many years. Rural areas are less well served
by elementary schools than urban areas and the regional variations
noticeable in other respects are also present in this regard. Not every

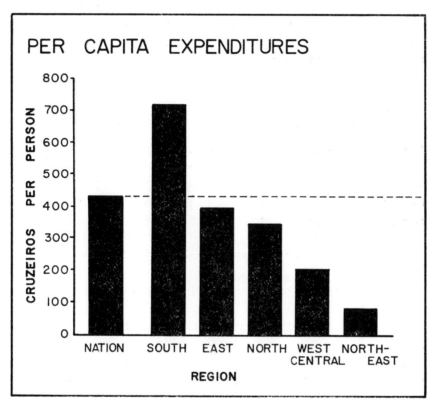

Fig. 6—Amount Budgeted Per Capita for Education, by Region, 1960.

child attends an elementary school, but most children at least gain
admission to the elementary levels of instruction and remain in
elementary schools for some years. Nearly 90 percent of elementary
students are in publicly supported schools, thus the economic limitations so obvious in the case of secondary education operate only
indirectly in primary education, as costs of clothes or transportation
or the loss of possible earnings by the child may affect attendance.
In 1964, approximately two-thirds of all Brazilian children between

the ages of seven and eleven attended school. In the South this proportion reached nearly three-quarters. In urban areas, the corresponding percentage rose to more than 80 (Table 2). It seems like, if for no other reason than that the urban population is increasing at a rate that greatly exceeds that of the rural population, that attendance at elementary schools will become virtually universal in the not too distant future.

Table 2

PERCENT OF CHILDREN AGED 7–11 ATTENDING
SCHOOL, BY REGION AND RESIDENCE, 1964

Residence	Nation	North	North-east	East[c]	South	West Central
Total	66.2	69.7	52.6	65.6	73.8	71.5
Urban[a]	81.0	87.6	78.5	79.5	83.4	78.2
Rural	51.4	54.1[b]	37.3	48.1	64.6	51.1[d]

[a]Includes population of "cidades" and "vilas."
[b]Enumeration incomplete in territories of Rondonia and Roraima and states of Pará and Amazonas.
[c]Does not include Guanabara (Rio de Janeiro).
[d]No data gathered in rural portions of Goiás. Enumeration incomplete in Mato Grosso.

The effectiveness of primary education is seriously hampered, however, by the small proportion of students who complete their primary schooling. This result is only in part due to dropouts. Most children of primary school age attend school. The low survival rates are principally due to a high proportion of failures. Of 1,200,000 children who enrolled in the first year primary in 1945 only 4 percent finished the fourth grade without repeating one or more years.[4] In 1962, only 56 percent of students enrolled in the first grade were promoted to the second. Promotion rates were substantially higher in the second, third, and fourth grades, but even so, 15 percent of fourth grade students were failed (Figure 7). One effect of this situation is a considerable bunching or piling up of children in the

[4]Werebe, *Grandezas e Misérias do Ensino Brasileiro*, 100. Data from a study by Moysés Kessel, "A Evasão Escolar," *Revista Brasileira de Estudos Pedagógicos*, No. 56, pp. 53–72.

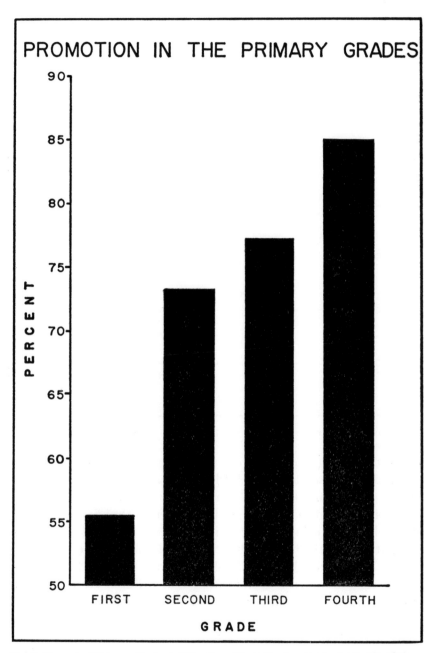

Fig. 7—Percent of Primary Students Who Passed to Following Grade, by Grade, 1962.

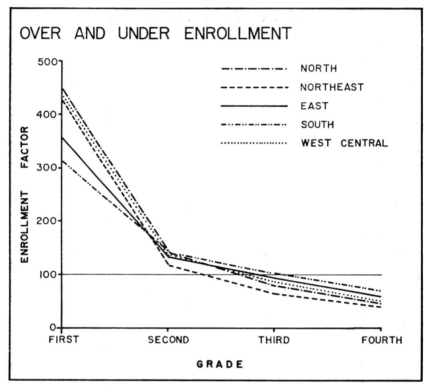

Fig. 8—Primary School Enrollment Factors by Grade, for Regions, 1962.

first and second grades who are overage in grade, with a corresponding under representation of children of grade age in the third and
fourth grades. In 1962 there were, in the nation as a whole, 355
children enrolled in the first grade for every 100 of first grade age,
even when including children six and seven years of age in the
computation of the figure. This enrollment factor was even higher
in the North, Northeast and West Central regions. Enrollment
factors remain above 100, indicating that children are overage in
grade through the second grade, and then drop below 100 in the
third and fourth grades (Figure 8). More than half of all primary
students in Brazil were enrolled in the first grade in 1962.

Among the numerous consequences of this state of affairs is, first of all, a glutting of the first grade and other primary grades with overage students who should be more advanced in their studies, limiting the number of places that may be occupied by children who reach school age. Were the failure rate in the first grade cut in half, room would be made in the schools for an additional two million or more students. The effects on the child are numerous, leading very frequently to discouragement and eventual dropping out. The cost of what amounts to extending primary instruction by one or more years for a majority of students is great, and the resources this represents could be better applied in alternative ways.

The proposition that nearly one-half of all children who enter primary school lack the intellectual capacity to acquire a knowledge of first grade-level materials during the year is untenable. The reasons for this situation must be sought elsewhere. Among the reasons enumerated by Werebe are: excessively rigorous promotion standards, "culturally" deprived children, poor physical facilities, insufficiently trained and indifferent teachers, poor school administration, and the theoretical orientation given to learning—with one exception, causes that lie with the school and educational system and not with the child.[5] Brazil cannot long afford the wastefulness of human resources which this system represents. Profound changes, especially in the organization, orientation, teacher training, and other aspects of primary instruction, are needed before this segment of the educational institution will be able to realize its full value as a factor contributing to the effective and rapid modernization of Brazilian society.

SECONDARY EDUCATION

Perhaps the most important observation to be derived from the statistics on secondary school enrollments is their relationship both as cause and as effect of the increasing upward social mobility that is coming to characterize Brazilian society. Another aspect of this phenomenon lies in the massive rural-urban migration which brings

[5]Werebe, *Grandezas e Misérias do Ensino Brasileiro*, 103–104.

large numbers of people into contact with educational opportunities by transferring them to urban centers.

That large numbers of Brazilians have come to the conclusion that a secondary education is not only desirable for their children but worth considerable personal sacrifice in order to achieve is undeniable. It would be my guess that a national sample survey would reveal that a large percentage of Brazilians place a high valuation on this kind of instruction. During the decade 1940–50 and again during 1950–60, secondary enrollments increased by more than 100 percent. During the first of these decades the increase in secondary enrollments was 5.5 times that of the population ten to nineteen years old, and during the second decade the comparable figure was 3.3 (Table 3). Especially striking were the enrollment gains vis-à-vis population made in the Eastern region during the 1940's and in the Northeast during the 1950's.

In spite of these spectacular advances, in 1960 only 7.5 percent of the population aged ten to nineteen, which closely corresponds to that of secondary school age, was enrolled in secondary schools. The enormous regional differences in educational opportunity were reflected in the range of this index which varied, in 1960, from 3.9 for the Northeastern region to 10.5 for the Southern region (Figure 9). Nevertheless, this percentage more than doubled in every region of Brazil between 1940 and 1960.

Although rapid increases in enrollment occurred in all types of secondary schools, the academic institutions which attempt to impart a humanistic liberal education to their charges, and the normal school which has a similar function restricted to a largely female enrollment, are odds-on favorites. During the postwar years, schools providing instruction in commerce, industrial arts, and agriculture at the secondary level lagged behind in their rate of increase and especially in total enrollment (Figure 10). For the period from 1960 to 1964, however, there was a sharp rise in the rate of increase of enrollments in both industrial and agricultural secondary curricula. Industrial enrollments experienced a particularly sharp rise, reflecting the increased job and income earning opportunities available to their graduates as well as the accelerating industrialization

Table 3

PERCENT OF THE POPULATION 10–19 YEARS OLD ENROLLED
IN SECONDARY SCHOOLS AND PERCENT CHANGE IN THE
POPULATION 10–19 AND IN SECONDARY ENROLLMENT
BY REGION, 1940, 1950, 1960

| Region | Percent Increase of Population Aged 10–19 and of Secondary School Enrollment | | | | b/a. 100 | |
| | 1940–50 | | 1950–60 | | | |
	Population (a)	Enrollment (b)	Population (a)	Enrollment (b)	1940–50	1950–60
Nation	20.9	114.2	33.1	111.2	5.5	3.3
North	24.7	92.8	38.8	116.1	3.8	3.0
Northeast	20.2	89.8	26.8	139.8	4.4	5.2
East	17.0	111.9	27.4	97.6	6.6	3.7
South	23.7	123.0	39.6	112.2	5.2	2.8
West Central	40.1	146.8	70.7	195.2	3.7	2.8

of the nation. This trend may in part be a reflection of the possibility that graduates of these schools now have of entering universities.

This increase is, however, contrary to the long-run trend for the
postwar decades which witnessed a 434 percent increase in secondary
academic enrollments, an 821 percent increase in normal school
enrollments, but smaller increases in technical courses, so that academic and normal school enrollments increased their share of the
total, while technical school enrollments dropped from 27 to 18 percent of the total. When secondary education became available to
increasing numbers of Brazilians, most of them chose the traditional
academic curriculum over what might be termed "modern" technical studies (Table 4).

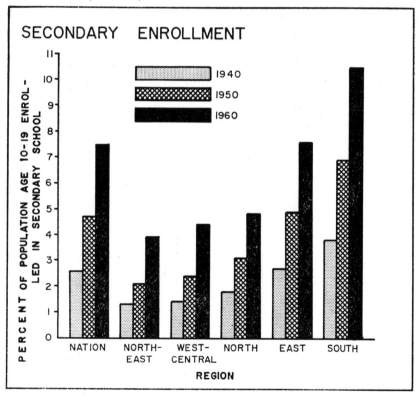

Fig. 9—Percent of the Population 10-19 Years Old Enrolled in Secondary Schools, by
Region, 1940, 1950, and 1960.

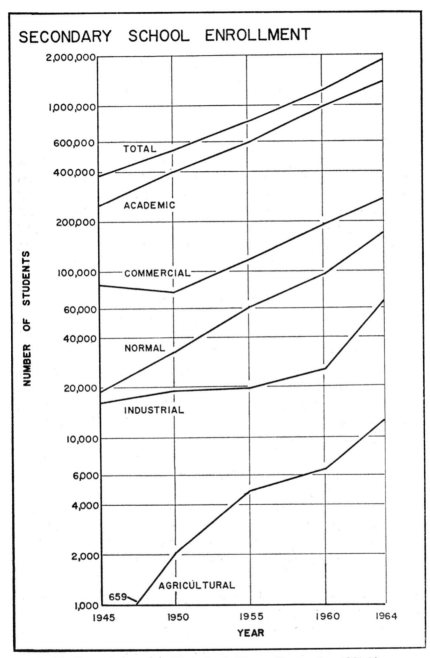

Fig. 10—Enrollment in Secondary Education by Types of Instruction, 1945–64.

Table 4

ENROLLMENT IN SECONDARY EDUCATION
NUMBER AND PERCENT, BY TYPE
OF INSTRUCTION, 1945–64

Type of Instruction	Enrollment 1945	1964	Percent Change	Percent of Total 1945	1964
Total	377,866	1,892,724	402	100.0	100.0
Academic	256,467	1,368,177	434	67.9	72.3
Technical	101,866	349,150	343	26.8	18.4
Industrial	16,674	68,819	314	4.4	3.6
Commercial	84,533	270,036	221	22.4	14.3
Agricultural	659	10,295	1,462	0.2	0.5
Normal	19,533	175,347	821	5.2	9.3

HIGHER EDUCATION

The transformation undergone by higher education since the 1930's has been considerable. Enrollments have increased at a rapid rate and the distribution of students among the several fields of study has undergone profound changes. Structural and other deficiencies have, however, been only partly remedied or not at all. Universities still are, by and large, in the words of a commission that reported in 1932, "a mere encampment where students and professors have fleeting encounters for classes and examinations that are also fleeting and hurried." [6] Full-time professors and full-time students are still the exception rather than the rule. The abuses of the lifetime chair or *cátedra* have proven highly resistant to correction and the system which breeds them impervious to reform. If the teaching function is vitiated, the research function is almost completely neglected. A recent study conducted in Rio by the Social Science Institute of the University of Brazil reports: "The conditions under which a Brazilian university professor lives are of the worst kind. Salaries are unattractive; they are very low, not permitting, through dependence on them alone, the maintenance of an up-to-date personal library nor, indeed, the payment of the normal expenses of the

[6]"Situação do Ensino no Brasil . . . ," *Jornal do Brasil,* March 13, 1966, p. 20.

head of a middle class family in contemporary Brazilian society. The professor is forced to balance his budget through an interminable accumulation or unfolding of activities." [7] Serious research under these conditions is extremely difficult.

In spite of the extensive catalog of ills that afflict Brazilian higher

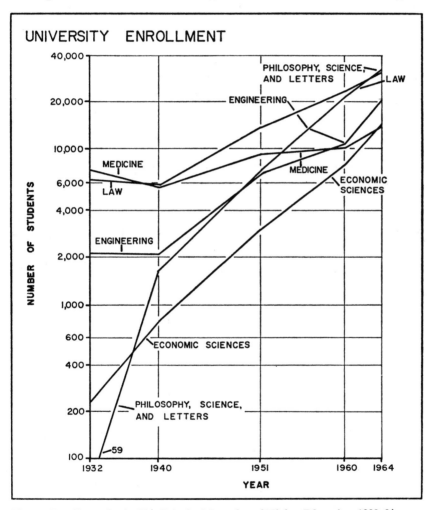

Fig. 11—Enrollment in the Five Principal Branches of Higher Education, 1932–64.

[7] *Ibid.*

education, it is unquestionably having a considerable impact on the society and its modernization. Engineers, physicians, economists, and the rest, even though trained under less than satisfactory conditions, are nevertheless being graduated at an accelerating rate. The expansion of enrollments has been truly phenomenal. The number of students pursuing degrees in engineering, economic sciences, and the various disciplines included under philosophy, science, and letters have skyrocketed since 1932 (Figure 11). Law and medicine, the traditional studies of the upper class, have lost the undisputed supremacy they possessed in the 1930's, and philosophy, science, and letters, which in 1932 had a negligible enrollment, had more students enrolled in 1964 than the faculties of law and far more than the faculties of medicine. From among the five major university courses—philosophy, law, engineering, medicine, and economic sciences—the big enrollment gains were made in those faculties which largely represent new approaches and are, to some extent at least, educational innovations. Thus, while enrollments in higher education as a whole increased by 608 percent between 1940 and 1964, engineering, philosophy, and economic sciences made far larger enrollment gains. Furthermore, it was the specialized branches of engineering such as chemical, mechanical, and elec-

Table 5

ENROLLMENT IN THE FIVE PRINCIPAL BRANCHES
OF HIGHER EDUCATION AND PERCENT
CHANGE, 1940–64

Course of Study	Enrollment		Percent of Total		Percent Change
	1940	1964	1940	1964	1940–64
Total	15,909	112,641	100.0	100.0	608
Law	5,793	30,974	36.4	27.5	435
Medicine	5,548	14,183	34.9	12.6	155
Engineering	2,172	20,728	13.7	18.4	834
Philosophy, Science and Letters	1,622	32,396	10.2	28.8	1,897
Economic Sciences	774	14,360	4.9	12.7	1,755

trical, rather than the traditional civil engineering, that were responsible for virtually all of the increase in enrollment in that field (Table 5). While law and medicine enrolled 71 percent of the students in these subjects in 1940, by 1964 that percentage had dropped to 40.

It is evident, in spite of increased enrollments, that the resources which Brazil invests in higher education are being underutilized. In 1964, even though the number of candidates for admission to institutions of higher learning outnumbered openings by 2 to 1, only 43 percent passed the infamous vestibular examinations, resulting in 14 percent of the openings, nationwide, going unfilled (Table 6). Indeed, as the number of candidates per opening increases, it would seem that many faculties make the vestibular examinations correspondingly more difficult, so that their function is one of exclusion rather than of selection of students.

Two fields, most notably, attracted applicants considerably in excess of openings: medicine with a ratio of 7.3 to 1 and non-civil engineering fields with a ratio of 4.2 to 1. In these subjects, even though the percentage of candidates that passed the vestibular examinations was exceedingly low, the number passed exceeded the number of openings in the universities, resulting in the so-called *excedentes* who rightfully agitate for the admission to which they are entitled but are denied for lack of openings.

Although the competition for places in faculties of philosophy is not nearly as keen, they have experienced the greatest growth in enrollment. This has been largely due to their function as a training ground for middle-class girls who take degrees that qualify them for secondary school teaching, much as the normal school does at the secondary level, preparing girls for primary school teaching. Sixty-five percent of their enrollment is of the female sex, and 50 percent of all women students in Brazilian higher education pursue courses offered by the faculties of philosophy.[8]

[8]Computed from data in I.B.G.E. (Instituto Brasileiro de Geografia e Estatística), *Sinópse Estatística do Ensino Superior, 1964* (Rio de Janeiro: Ministério de Educação e Cultura, 1965), 44. The following courses are offered in faculties of philosophy, science, and letters: social science, philosophy, physics, geography, history, natural history, various branches of language and literature, mathematics, education, chemistry, astronomy, drawing, geology, meteorology, and psychology.

Table 6

OPENINGS IN INSTITUTIONS OF HIGHER
LEARNING, NUMBER OF CANDIDATES FOR
ADMISSION, PERCENT OF CANDIDATES
PASSED, PERCENT OF OPENINGS FILLED, AND
CANDIDATES PER OPENING, BY
COURSE OF STUDY, 1964

| Course of Study | Number of Openings | Candidates | | Percent of Openings Filled | Candidates per Opening |
		Number	Percent Passed		
All Courses	56,464	112,485	43.2	86.0	2.0
Philosophy, Science, and Letters	20,486	18,880	60.7	56.0	0.9
Law	7,620	17,112	49.3	110.7	2.2
All Engineering	6,556	24,719	31.2	117.7	3.8
Civil Engineering	1,238	2,180	50.0	88.0	1.8
Other Engineering	5,318	22,539	29.4	124.6	4.2
Economics	3,608	7,137	51.3	101.6	2.0
Medicine	3,036	22,151	16.9	123.2	7.3
Dentistry	2,188	3,706	50.2	85.1	1.7
Agronomy	1,256	2,703	44.2	89.1	2.2
Social Work	1,413	1,455	68.2	70.5	1.0
Administration	1,320	2,654	33.8	68.0	2.0
Architecture	690	1,480	44.8	96.1	2.1
Pharmacy	1,095	1,394	55.8	71.1	1.3
Art, Drama & Music	1,210	698	84.0	48.4	0.6
Veterinary Science	689	1,264	49.4	90.6	1.8
Nursing	782	434	73.0	40.5	0.6
Others	4,515	6,698	83.8	124.3	1.5

Nursing, on the other hand, a profession essential for the most effective functioning of health services and the fullest utilization of health facilities and personnel was, along with art, drama, and music, the least sought-after course of study. Only 434 applicants took exams for the 782 vacancies in nursing schools in 1964, and, of these, more than one-fourth were failed. The image of the nurse as a servant and the connotation of lax morality given to intimate contact with members of the opposite sex make this an unattractive profession to most Brazilian girls. Students of medicine outnumber students of nursing by about 10 to 1. The long-run deleterious effect of this situation on the provision of the medical services which a modern industrial society requires is impossible to evaluate but will certainly be great.

Relative shifts in enrollment between what might be termed traditional subjects, such as law and medicine, to modern subjects, such as economics and the specialized branches of engineering, may be examined by comparing enrollment trends for the fields which fall into these two groups. In the following discussion two definitions of traditional and modern will be used. Definition A includes in the traditional category, philosophy, science and letters, law, civil engineering, and dentistry; the modern category comprises non-civil engineering, economics, agronomy, social work, administration, and architecture. Together these fields accounted for more than 90 percent of the students enrolled in 1964. Since some argument is possible over the inclusion of philosophy, science, and letters—a very large and heterogeneous category—in the traditional group, definition B places it in the modern category, although most of its enrollment occurs in such traditional majors as pedagogy and literature. Whichever definition is used, enrollment gains in modern subjects outstripped those in traditional subjects between 1953 and 1964 (Table 7), and the percentage of students enrolled in modern subjects increased while that of students enrolled in traditional subjects decreased. Using definition A, the proportional share that modern courses claimed of the enrollment doubled from 16 to 32 percent during the decade in question.

This heartening shift in enrollments, along with the implications that it has for a modernizing society, is less a function of the changing educational goals and value orientation of Brazilian youth than of the distribution of openings in the several fields of study. Were all applicants for admission to universities successful in gain-

Table 7

ENROLLMENT TRENDS IN TRADITIONAL AND
MODERN COURSES OF STUDY IN INSTITUTIONS OF
HIGHER LEARNING, 1953–64

Type	Number Enrolled		Index (1953 = 100)		Percent of total	
	1953	1964	1953	1964	1953	1964
Definition A[a]						
Traditional	45,638	88,502	100	194	83.8	67.9
Modern	8,830	41,816	100	474	16.2	32.1
Definition B[b]						
Traditional	37,698	58,596	100	155	68.8	45.0
Modern	17,670	71,722	100	406	31.9	55.0

[a]Traditional includes: Philosophy, science, letters, law, civil engineering, and dentistry; modern includes: non-civil engineering, economics, agronomy, social work, administration, and architecture.
[b]Same as definition A except that Philosophy, science, and letters is considered modern.

Table 8

PERCENT OF STUDENTS ENROLLED IN MODERN
AND TRADITIONAL COURSES AND PERCENT OF
CANDIDATES SEEKING
ADMISSION TO MODERN AND
TRADITIONAL COURSES, 1964

Type of Course	Definition A[a]		Definition B[b]	
	Enrollment	Candidates	Enrollment	Candidates
Modern	32.1	20.0	55.0	42.5
Traditional	67.9	80.0	45.0	57.5

ing admission to the faculties to which they apply, 80 percent of
them would be pursuing traditional courses under definition A and
58 percent under definition B (Table 8). That the distribution of
enrollments is different represents the effects of a choice forced on
the students. Universities, then, much more than other branches of

education, are exercising leadership in the provision of the skills deemed essential to the modernization of the society.

SOCIALIZATION IN THE SCHOOL

An important share of the process of socialization through which a child acquires the basic psychological attributes and characteristics of a member of his nation, social class, and sex takes place in the school. Along with the family and play and neighborhood groups, the school molds the personality by defining roles, their expectations, and by exacting conformity in some degree to normative and role-stipulated behavior. Does the impact of the Brazilian school on the personality of the child develop traits conducive to innovativeness, analytical reasoning, and self-reliance? Are these traits important for the stimulation and acceptance of modernizing social change? The answer to both of these questions must be begged, and instead the tentative hypothesis advanced that Brazilian schools, especially at the primary level where their impact on personality development is greatest, tend to stifle rather than develop the personality traits on which modernization depends, and from which the society must draw its innovators.

Several accounts have been rendered concerning what might be termed the psycho-social environment of the Brazilian primary school. In general terms the ability to verbalize patterned or structured responses to questions is stressed and rewarded; the child's freedom both in a physical and intellectual sense is restricted within narrow limits, and the teacher views his own role mainly as one of drilling set answers to set questions into his pupils. Memorization is emphasized at the expense of understanding. According to J. Roberto Moreira, the teacher, given his working conditions,

is not, and cannot be an orienter of school activities . . . he is above all a censor and distributor of tasks; he behaves as a controller, always at the front of the class, distributing work, questioning, demanding, punishing frequently and rewarding rarely, even so inadequately, for he does it by establishing discriminations or parallels of opposition of supposed individual values . . . . In such an environment and before such a censor, the pupils must behave according to predetermined standards whose functionality neither they nor their teacher understand . . . . The common rule of this behavior was the silence of the pupils except in oral lessons. In addition to silence the pupil should remain seated during all the lessons being allowed to get up only with the express permission of the teacher.[9]

If we accept as probably true the hypothesis that modernization depends, among other things, on individuals endowed with innovativeness, analytical reasoning ability, and other such traits, then it would seem that Brazilian primary schools are not contributing to modernization, by developing these necessary traits in the population. This is not to say that the effect of the primary school on modernization is negative. Impressive evidence can be marshalled with which to argue that education is a precondition of modernization however undesirable some of its characteristics may be.[10] It would seem, however, that the contribution of Brazilian primary and secondary schools to the modernization of the society could be greatly magnified by appropriate measures to restructure and reorient the educational process.

Empirical data that bear upon these questions are practically nonexistent. A fairly recent study by Bernard C. Rosen does, however, provide evidence that a number of traits conducive to modernization are less prevalent in Brazil than in the United States.[11] Since these traits are developed to some extent at least in the school, it seems safe to assume that the school plays a role, probably important, in their relative absence. An American sample and a Brazilian sample of school boys was studied and the data were controlled for social class. Results showed consistently higher scores of achieve-

[9]*Introdução ao Estudo do Curriculo da Escola Primária. CILEME,* Pub. No. 7 (1955) , 164, quoted in Werebe, *Grandezas e Miserias do Ensino Brasileiro,* 88.

[10]Cf. Paul Montavon, "Some Questions on Education and Economic Development," and Martin Carnoy, "Education in Latin America: An Empirical Approach," in *Viewpoints on Education and Social Change in Latin America* (University of Kansas: Center of Latin American Studies, 1965) , 23–38, 41–54. Also, S. N. Eisenstadt, *Modernization: Protest and Change* (Englewood Cliffs, N.J.: Prentice-Hall, 1966) , 16–18; Theodore W. Schultz, *The Economic Value of Education* (New York: Columbia University Press, 1963) .

[11]Bernard C. Rosen, "The Achievement Syndrome and Economic Growth in Brazil," *Social Forces,* Vol. XLII (March, 1964) , 341–54.

ment motivation and achievement values for American boys. Other data led the author to conclude that the Brazilians in his sample "are more fatalistic, place less emphasis upon planning and the postponement of gratifications, put a lower evaluation on work, and are less willing to be mobile physically in order to take advantage of better job opportunities." [12] These and other studies are highly tentative. More needs to be known about the relationship of education and the school to modernization; knowledge upon which far reaching educational and economic policy decisions could be based.

Sources of Figures and Tables

Fig. 1. I.B.G.E. (Instituto Brasileiro de Geografia e Estatística), VII Recenseamento Geral do Brasil, 1960, *Censo Demográfico, Resultados Preliminares,* Série Especial, II, (Rio de Janeiro: Serviço Nacional de Recenseamento, 1965), 2.

Fig. 2. *Ibid.*

Fig. 3. S.E.E.C. (Serviço Estatístico da Educação e Cultura), *Sinópse Estatística do Ensino Superior, 1964* (Rio de Janeiro: Ministério da Educaçao e Cultura, 1965), xiv, xi.

Fig. 4. Data from official sources in Ministério da Educaçao e Cultura, made available through the courtesy of Anísio Teixeira.

Fig. 5. I.B.G.E., *Anuário Estatístico do Brasil, 1955, 1962, and 1965.* (Rio de Janeiro: Conselho Nacional de Estatística, 1955, 1962, and 1965), 432; 282, 287; and 427; respectively. All enrollment figures are those for the beginning of the school year *(matrícula geral)* . Secondary enrollments for the sake of comparability exclude nonacademic curricula. Inclusion of nonacademic secondary enrollments raises the 1964 figure to twenty-four largely as a result of the rapid increase in these enrollments, especially between 1960 and 1964.

Fig. 6. I.B.G.E., *Anuário, 1961 and 1965,* 383 and 32–33, respectively.

Fig. 7. I.B.G.E., *Anuário, 1964,* 339–40.

Fig. 8. *Ibid.*

Fig. 9. I.B.G.E., *Censo Demografico* (1960), *passim; Anuário,* (1956), 41; *Censo Demografico* (1940), Série Nacional, II (Rio de Janeiro: Serviço Gráfico do I.B.G.E., 1950), *passim.* Figures for the West Central and Northern regions for 1960 are based on my estimates of the population aged 10–19 for that year.

Fig. 10. S.E.E.C., *Sinópse Estatística do Ensino Médio, 1964* (Rio de Janeiro: Ministério da Educaçao e Cultura, 1965), 4.

Fig. 11. See Figure 4 above.

Table 1. S.E.E.C., *Ensino Superior,* xiv and *Ensino Médio,* xi.

Table 2. I.N.E.P. (Instituto Nacional de Estudos Pedagógicos), *Censo Escolar do Brasil, Resultados Preliminares.* (Rio de Janeiro: I.B.G.E.–Comissão Central do Censo Escolar, 1965), Table 1.

Table 3. See Figure 9 above.

Table 4. S.E.E.C., *Ensino Médio,* 4.

Table 5. See Figure 4 above.

Table 6. S.E.E.C., *Ensino Superior,* 1–2.

Table 7. *Ibid.,* xiii (unnumbered) .

Table 8. *Ibid.*

[12] *Ibid.,* 353–54.

The Geography of Brazil's Modernization and Implications for the Years 1980 and 2000 A.D.

Kempton E. Webb

IN THIS PAPER I SHALL TRY TO (1) DEFINE THE TERM "MODERNIZA-tion" from a geographic point of view, and (2) propose a method of analyzing the geography of modernization in Brazil. A further objective will be an attempt to project this analysis to the years 1980 and 2000 in order to anticipate what the geography of Brazil will look like. What is being sought is an historical geography projected ahead in time.

The conclusions of this paper comprise projections of processes of physical and cultural change through time, and may be stated as an hypothesis. In short, what I see in Brazil's future is a junction or coincidence around the year 2000 A.D. of two distinct sets of processes which are only loosely related in the latter 1960's: (1) the process of physical, and therefore economic, integration through a road network expansion and, (2) the process of industrialization and economic growth, which in the mid-1960's is as yet limited in scope and area within Brazil.

The search for a methodology for the study of a geography of modernization is useful and interesting for at least four reasons: (1) it is valuable in terms of identifying and evaluating the processes as they now operate and in terms of the components which comprise them, (2) such a study would contribute to the knowledge of particular areas of Brazil, (3) there may be general value in whatever methodological innovations may be the result of such a study, and (4) such an approach has potentially far-reaching implications and applications of a very practical nature in planning and regional development efforts. Time passes at an extremely rapid rate in Brazil in that ten or fifteen years is a very long interval during which many things can happen and can alter the landscape in fundamental ways. It is possible that if some of the undesirable outcomes which are predicted for the coming decades are indicated now, steps may be taken in order to delay or even avoid them. This is the pragmatic dimension of a study of the geography of modernization.

There are many definitions of the term modernization, and I shall not try to present a review of them since this has been done by others.[1] It is obvious, however, that any discussion of modernization requires that the term be defined clearly by its user.

Modernization from a geographic point of view can be defined as the process which involves the valorization of land or areas which is accompanied by increasing levels of productivity and which includes elements of long-term gain to the area, to its present and future inhabitants, and to the nation of which it is a part. It is a concept which involves constantly accruing benefits to the land, to the area, and to its people. This long-term aspect contrasts with the short-term valorization typical of the hollow frontier which has characterized much of Brazil's history of settlement.[2]

PROCESSES

The key to the study of geographic aspects of modernization is accurate identification of the kinds of processes which shape the landscape. These are both natural processes, independent of man, and cultural processes, which are direct results of his consciously or unconsciously motivated action.

[1]C.E. Black, *The Dynamics of Modernization: A Study in Comparative History* (New York: Harper & Row, 1966) .

[2]Preston E. James has described and analyzed the "hollow frontier" of Brazil in his monumental *Latin America* (New York: The Odyssey Press, scheduled for publication in 1969) .

Let us distinguish two basic sets of processes. On one level a distinction could be made between physical processes of landscape change and, on the other, cultural processes of landscape change. Nevertheless, a more meaningful and more usable classification might be better presented in terms of unconscious processes of landscape change versus conscious processes of landscape change. In this second distinction we find that there are physical and cultural elements in both categories.

What are some examples of processes of landscape change which are independent of man's conscious control on a mass level? One instance which is particularly evident in Brazil is the process of deforestation and its far-reaching results of erosion and stream silting. The *devastação das matas* is an historic and geographic fact which does not loom largely in the literature of Brazil but which is one of those eminently unnewsworthy realities of life which is evident in almost every inhabited part of the country and which has an impact, direct or indirect, upon the lives of all Brazilians. While it is true that this is a phenomenon which is the result of man's individual overt actions, it is ultimately the gross sum of these millions of individual acts which has brought, and is continuing to bring, such havoc to the Brazilian land. From sheet erosion and gullying in crop lands, to road and bridge wash outs, to the flooding of urban slums, the manifestations of deforestation and resultant increases of rainfall runoff are evident. This is the bitter harvest of four hundred years of repeated forest destruction on sloping land.

Briefly, what has happened throughout Brazil's history is that the settlers were attracted to the richer soils associated with the semideciduous evergreen forests, coinciding with what is now the most populated coastal fringe of the country. Because of their attractiveness to *caboclo* farmers, the areas were opened up and the trees cut down in order to plant either subsistence crops or, in São Paulo's case, cash crops such as coffee. The absence of conservation practices, which are still lacking in all but the most agriculturally productive parts of southern Brazil, meant that continued deforestation, overcropping and overgrazing on sloping land, resulted in widespread erosion which has carried off untold millions of tons of humus-rich topsoil into the rivers and represents an incalculable loss to Brazil's productive capacities.

In the twentieth century, with the larger populations and more efficient tools, the process of deforestation has accelerated and its effects are more serious. The haunting question is, how much longer can this continue? The limit has already been reached in some of the very steeply sloping areas of the Serra do Mar, north of Rio, and in southern Minas Gerais where overcropping and overgrazing for over three hundred years has removed not only the original *mata* forest but also every vestige of soil so that today only the bare bones of Mother Earth are evident in the broad expanses of exposed granite and gneiss bedrock.

A second example of unconscious processes is that of population growth, which in Brazil has risen to the extraordinarily high level of around 3.5 percent per year in 1967 from a rate of 2.4 percent in 1956. Again, this is a fact of life which is not determined by national policy or by decision-making in higher levels. It is simply the net effect of a myriad of individual decisions, or maybe lack of decisions, whereby a high birthrate has been coupled with a lowered deathrate, due to the introduction of medical technology, producing a very high increment of growth in the middle years of the twentieth century. A geographic approach to the study of population growth would give attention to the disparities between different areas in terms of population growth characteristics. Which areas are growing fastest in population? Why? Where are the stagnant areas? Where are those of declining population? There are some in Brazil, but not many, to be sure.[3]

A further example of processes which are the result of unconscious mass decisions is the process of internal migration whereby

[3]Several illuminating parts of a group research project by Brazilian geographers have been published recently:
   a. Maria Emilia Teixeira de Castro Botelho, "Ritmos de Crescimento Urbano do Nordeste," *Revista Brasileira de Geografia*, XXVII, No. 3 (Julho-Sept, 1965), 484–90.
   b. Ariadne Soares Souto Mayor, Solange Tietzmann Silva, and Elizabeth Fortunata Gentile, "Crecimento Media Anual da População do Nordeste Periodos de 1920 a 1950 e de 1950 a 1960," *Revista Brasileira de Geografia* XXVII, No. 2 (Abril-Junho, 1965), 295–304.

sizeable numbers of people move from one area to another, such as from the Northeast of Brazil to São Paulo. Brazil has a long and interesting history of internal migrations, some of which have been the result of official policy, such as the transport of drought-fleeing *flagellados* from the Northeast during the last century to the Amazon, or the ill-fated colonization schemes in this decade in Maranhão in the Middle North. The great bulk of the internal migration of Brazilians, however, has been spontaneous, whereby an individual simply picks up his family and moves, whether by bus, by truck, or by foot, from one part of the country to another.

One distinction can be made regarding the actual numbers of people involved in the internal migrations. Another distinction can be made concerning the quality of the migratory stream or the *quality* of the population. In the 1960's we witness, as a result of the general westward movement of population, the shifting of agricultural entrepreneurs, especially *fazendeiros* or cattle raisers, into the remote area of Pará state. It is reasonable to expect that one entrepreneur with capital at his disposal will bring more change than many average Northeastern *caboclos* or poor migrants whose only capital is their muscles, the sweat of their brows, and their readiness to face great risks and hardship in return for a chance to succeed.

The rural-to-urban movement is a general phenomenon throughout Brazil, and while planners, *politicos,* and intellectuals talk about whether or not it is desirable, the fact remains that the tide of movement is unstemmable. People cannot and will not be stopped in their trek to the city, seeking new opportunities.

A fourth example might be the market prices of common commodities of items for personal consumption such as food. While there is some evidence that monopolistic practices have influenced prices in one place or another, most enterprises have insufficient power to affect prices on a wide scale. Therefore, one might cite market prices and the practice of fixing market prices as something which is out of the control of the individual, and, rather, is a general response to conditions of supply and demand and competition.

These examples are only four out of many which might be cited which illustrate a number of processes or phenomena which proceed and operate independently of man's conscious decisions on a broad scale. These are the kinds of things which go on regardless of which man or political party is in power and regardless of Brazil's balance of payments situation or her current diplomatic relations. These are the things that are generally not the subjects of learned treatises, yet in their own invisible way, they are very much a part of the fabric of everyday life in Brazil and certainly a part of the mainstream of Brazil's cultural history and cultural geography.

Let us now look at a number of more obvious examples of processes and features which are the result of man's conscious thought and action and usually the results of decision-making on a large organizational level.

The construction of roads in the mid-twentieth century is a highly organized activity which is beyond the realm of the individual man on the land. There are federal, state, and *municipio* plans for roads, and the tendency has been toward integration and coordination of all levels of plans into a comprehensive and sensible strategy which has as its goal the physical integration of practically all parts of the Brazilian national territory. The importance of roads in the developing countries cannot be overestimated. It is usually underrated since many people regard them more as engineering feats than as the revolutionary agents of economic and social change.

It is appropriate then to pause and examine the official Brazilian government plan for highway development. I refer to the *Plano Nacional de Viação, Setor Rodoviaria* published by the Divisão de Planejamento and the Departamento Nacional de Estradas de Rodagem (DNER) in 1965. This is a remarkable document which is probably the single most important indicator of where and what Brazil will be in the year 2000 A.D. This assertion is based upon the fact that highways are the social and economic lifelines of the country, not railroads, which had a more important, though still limited, economic role in the late nineteenth and early twentieth centuries.

What does this map reveal? First of all, it indicates the categories of existing paved roads, existing unpaved roads, and of roads which are definitely planned for future construction. On the original map

further distinctions were made in terms of the improvements which
were planned for the period of 1966 and 1967. It is understood that
delays do occur, but that this is the general master plan, and that this
is what the roadmap of Brazil will, in all likelihood, be certainly

This map summarizes the more detailed original 1965 DNER map which
gave more emphasis to *(1)* roads to be constructed, *(2)* existing roads which
were to have been paved, and *(3)* new roads to be paved at the time of their
construction (as done for the Belo Horizonte-Brasilia highway). This map
shows the bold extensions of the highway network westward and northward
to incorporate the outermost areas of Brazil into the effective national territory.

by around 1980, which is closer than we realize. This map has more meaning to those who are familiar with the present and past distribution of roads in Brazil.

The present pattern of all-weather roads is limited mainly to the most densely populated zone about two hundred miles deep, inland from the Atlantic Ocean. Since the 1950's, beginning especially with the government of Juscelino Kubitschek, highways were extended and paved at a rate hitherto unequalled in Brazil's history. This policy of aggressive extension of transport routes to all corners of the country has been continued by subsequent governments.

What can we read from the map? In brief, one observes that: (1) there will be many more roads in Brazil than there are now; (2) there will be many more places and areas served by highways; (3) there will, as a natural result of this, be more intersections which will serve as local crossroads, market centers, storage depots, and governmental, political, and population foci; (4) there will be, furthermore, more pairs of alternate routes, as contrasted to the single trunk road which is still the general occurrence and not the exception in Brazil. The situation will be avoided where, as I witnessed in 1965, the heavy snows and rains in southern Brazil raised the level of the Pelotas River by 130 feet and destroyed the three-year-old, 380-foot-long bridge over it connecting Rio Grande do Sul and Santa Catarina, producing a virtually complete isolation of Rio Grande do Sul from the rest of Brazil. An alternate route is now under construction; (5) more of the roads will be paved, or at least of an all-weather type of construction and maintenance; and (6) there will also be more pioneer roads.

The map reveals a network or web which reaches out, amoeba-like, to touch and incorporate the remotest corners of the country, namely the territories of Roraima, Acre, and Rondonia with tributary roads reaching out to establish contact with the borders of Guyana, Venezuela, Colombia, Peru, Bolivia, and Paraguay.

The present work of DNER as revealed to me by an official of the DNER in Rio in February, 1967, is focused on (1) consolidating existing networks and improving existing roads; (2) extending the main axis roads to the farthest reaches of the national territory and linking them with the capital of Brasilia; (3) the building of connecting roads utilizing existing towns as the locations of crossroads; and (4) recognizing the Amazon River as part of the national circulation system of transportation. The end result of this extending network will be the valorization of land and, therefore, the valorization of production from that land because of the access of these places to local, national, and even to world markets. It should be added that, while the location of any given projected road route on the map may vary by several miles to one side or another, the connecting points of particular towns will remain as indicated.

A second example of man-made decisions and features is the airline network. Airline service is highly developed in Brazil. This is true in the remote areas precisely because of the unavailability or unsuitability of alternative modes of transportation. When a given area is unaccessible by land or water there tends to be a compensating access by air, and this includes not only passenger but also freight service as well.

A representative of the Air Ministry informed me in 1966 that Brazil is divided into two large regions in terms of the economics of air fares. In effect, those air routes to the east of and including a line connecting Belem and Brásilia, and following the Paraná River, pay their own way in terms of air revenues. On the other hand, the air service to the west of that line, the most sparsely populated part of the country, is heavily subsidized and the air service is not covered by the revenues it produces. What this means is that the air service is used as a conscious agent of settlement and development. Communications of outlying areas with the populous part of the country are subsidized by the federal government in the form of air service by both commercial lines and the Brazilian Air Force (FAB) with the hope that people will move into those areas, invest money, and make those places productive to the point where they may be able to sustain their own economic growth and justify better surface connections with Brazilian heartland.

It is obvious that there are many other kinds of actions which have an ultimate impact upon the land which are the product of man's collective conscious decisions and behavior. We need cite only the development policies undertaken by federal, state, local, and regional organizations such as SUDENE (Superintendency for the Development in the Northeast) and SUDAM (Superintendency for the Development of the Amazon) .

National decisions regarding special commodities such as sugar, coffee, and cacao may have an impact upon the landscape, as do decisions involving policies toward industries and whether they are or are not encouraged to go into certain areas.

The Areas

Let us now pass from some of the processes and kinds of actions which are relevant to the distribution of the modernization phenomenon to the actual geographic areas which are affected. We may ask, in effect, where does modernization occur? There are two primary kinds of areas: (1) the new pioneer areas and (2) the older traditional settled areas.

The most obvious areas where modernization can occur are the recent pioneer zones such as western Paraná, Matto Grosso, Amapá, along the Belem-Brasilia Highway, and in the remote areas of Pará state. The significant aspect of the pioneer zones is that they represent open land which is generally devoid of long history of ownership and legal encumbrances. These are the areas where a "development mentality" prevails, places where everything is new!—new land, new people, new possibilities, and a new landscape to be shaped. There are few, if any, crusts of traditional oligarchies which tend to hinder development efforts by their conservative thinking.

Pioneer lands do not necessarily mean areas where geographic modernization is occurring. The classic monograph by Pierre Mombeig, *Pioniers et Planteurs de São Paulo,* documents the sweep of population westward in search of new coffee lands across the state of São Paulo. In many instances, the land became exhausted and abandoned after the soils had ceased to produce suitable yields of coffee. It was the passage of a hollow frontier.

It appears that in Goias and other parts of the Centro-Oeste, the phenomenon of geographic modernization, and not a hollow frontier, is visible.[4] The high degree of commercialization of rice and other food production and of scientific farming generally, which is more typical of southern Brazil, is unique and promises long-term benefit to those areas.

In western Paraná, although it is hampered by conflicts over land titles, the pioneer activity there is especially interesting because it represents a confrontation of a southward moving front of traditional farming, peoples, and practices with a northwestward moving front of more technically advanced farmers from Rio Grande do Sul and Santa Catarina. It will be interesting to observe how the confrontation of these two different outlooks on farming and land will be resolved.

In Amapá, part of the revenues from ICOMI manganese mines are being wisely applied to the economic diversification of the local economy through the activities of IRDA (Instituto Regional do Desenvolvimento do Amapá). Commercial agricultural and lumbering are being carried on in the context of the latest scientific principals and research, and the field is wide open for the highest level innovation.

The other kind of area where modernization can occur, although usually with greater difficulty, is the more populated traditional areas such as Northeast Brazil. There, this means a rationalization of productions in the older, sometimes abandoned areas. Modernization further requires the provision of public services, roads, jobs, and education, and represents vast investments on local levels as well as the federal and state levels.

In the Northeast the problem seems to be further complicated by the existence of an established crust of opinion of dominant groups which have tended, historically, to hold back most types of reform and liberalization of land and society. It is ironic that there exist, even within the densely populated parts of Brazil, areas like the

[4]Paul Mandell, "Goiás as a Case Study" in *Brazil: Field Research Guide in the Social Sciences,* Institute of Latin American Studies, (New York: Columbia University Press, 1966) , 52–76.

broad flat *tabuleiros* north of Recife and the *Baixada Fluminense* near Rio which are sizeable tracts, sparsely populated, and which have the potential capacity to be more productively managed than they are. Much of this land is in the hands of large landowners who can hold onto them simply because land taxes are so low. A rigorously enforced discriminatory land tax law would make it uneconomic for them to retain large areas of land in an unproductive state.

If there is such a thing as a frontier of modernization in Brazil, where is it? Within the context of Brazilian history, it is safe to say that the initial influence of geographic modernization originated with European colonists in southern Brazil during the last half of the nineteenth century. The contemporary version of modernization originated in the Central West (Goias and Mato Grosso) and is largely a post-World War II phenomenon. The opening up and subsequent development of the Mato Grosso de Goiás near Anapolis in the 1940's (which is well documented by Speridião Faissol's monograph, *O Mato Grosso de Goiás* [Conselho Nacional de Geografia] and Robert Carmin) [5] and the subsequent planning and building of Brasilia came at a time when new approaches to the notion of area or regional development were being tried. The success of Belo Horizonte as the first Brazilian planned city (1897) and the apparent success of Brasilia (1960) were encouraging influences. It may be that the most profound impact of Brasilia upon the nation will be due to the fact that the city has become, by its interior location, the destination for principal trunk highways which are being built toward it from the coastal capitals. Without Brasilia, there would be little reason to build these radial spoke roads. Every new road becomes a ribbon of settlement as well as an axis of transportation and the foundation upon which subsequent development takes place.

The initial influence in the Central West, then, has probably had an impact upon the older areas such as the Northeast but it is not yet clear as to what direction the influence of geographic modernization may take there. To a large extent, the degree to which geographic

[5] Robert Carmin, *Anapolis, Brazil: Regional Capital of an Agricultural Frontier*, Dept. of Geography, Research Paper 35 (Chicago: University of Chicago Press, 1953).

modernization is possible depends greatly upon the ecological balance between the cities and their hinterlands. In Minas Gerais, for example, there now exists an admirable symbiotic and efficient relationship between the consuming center of Belo Horizonte and the various commodity procurement and storage depots scattered over the state.[6] There does not yet exist this organic balance between the cities and the countryside in areas like the Northeast.[7] In southern Brazil, especially São Paulo state, it does exist.

As for the frontier of modernization, we can suggest that one frontier is on an area basis in terms of the larger regions of the country, i.e. western Paraná, Amapá, along the Belem-Brasília highway, and in Goiás. These are all frontiers on an area basis. The other frontier of modernization can be thought of as scattered irradiating points or centers of innovation where the cities are the foci around which the valorization of land and sometimes an ecological harmony between city and hinterland are being established. Cities like Campina Grande in Paraíba and Curitiba in Paraná are outstanding examples of this second kind of frontier of geographic modernization.[8]

The cities are certainly loci of modernization, and not only of geographic modernization. The Brazilian government is using cities as instruments of change, and sometimes reform, as evidenced by the location of a new capital in the middle of the country. The economic development of the state of Bahia has been approached on the basis of using cities as spearheads of economic development in the various regions of that state. In this paper we are more concerned with cities as devices for bringing geographic modernization to larger areas.

INTERACTIONS AND PROJECTIONS

We have identified several categories of processes which can be viewed as interacting with each other and also interacting with the

[6]Kempton E. Webb, *Geography of Food Supply in Central Minas Gerais,* NAS-NRC. Foreign Field Report 4 (Washington, D.C., 1959), 110.

[7]Kempton E. Webb, *Suprimento de Generos Alimenticios para a Cidade de Fortaleza,* Banco do Nordeste do Brasil (Fortaleza, 1957), 146.

[8]Maria Francisca T.C. Cardoso, "Campina Grande e Sua Função como Capital Regional," *Revista Brasileira de Geografia,* XXV No. 4 (Out-Dez, 1963), 415–51.

areas in which they operate. One of our objectives was to project these interactions of processes in Brazil and peer into the future to see how the face of Brazil will look around the year 2000.

It seems to me that by 1980 there should exist widespread awareness in Brazil—as there already exists among some people such as geographers, planners, and ecologists—of the dominant role which Brazilians have over their habitat. More importantly, Brazilians, by then, will have the power and capacity to use their land and resources in rational ways for the long-term benefit to the nation. In short, Brazilians will realize and believe that they can not only master their habitat but that they can use it in ways which will be permanently beneficial to their whole society.

By the year 2000 we shall probably be able to witness the junction of these two fundamental processes mentioned earlier, namely the physical integration of the nation, mainly through the construction of highways and, secondly, the process of continuing economic growth and development. By the year 2000 it seems very likely that Brazil will emerge to the eyes of the rest of the world as a massive, viable, productive, functioning state whose effective national territory will approximate the total national territory. In 1967 the effective national territory was probably not much more than one-third of the total national territory.[9] By 2000 A.D. the effective national territory should comprise at least two-thirds of the total national territory. Effective national territory means that proportion of the total country's area which is productive in more than a subsistence sense and which contributes to the economic life of the entire nation. The existence of highways and of efficient communications will mean that the benefits of economic development and growth will have been carried to the remotest corners of the country and that the vast disparities of economic level from one area to another will decrease. In the mid-1960's it is still possible to move backward in time into the nineteenth and eighteenth centuries simply by traveling to different areas of Brazil.

The problem of accelerating deforestation, if not checked soon

[9]Preston E. James also formulated the concepts of total national territory and effective national territory.

by effective means of rational land management, will produce an expanding barren wasteland. This insidious and progressive "desertification" has already been observed in many areas of Brazil, especially in the Northeast.

Finally, we shall probably observe in 2000 an overlapping of hinterlands of the larger regional cities in somewhat the same way that the hinterlands of São Paulo and Rio de Janeiro overlap in the 1960's, as shown by the study *O Grande Região do Rio de Janeiro e a Sua Região* published in 1964 by the Conselho Nacional de Geografia. The overlapping of hinterlands will extend through the existing equivalent of the Latin American Free Trade Association (LAFTA) in 2000 A.D. so that the South American continent should be a much more viable and effective area. But only the growth of a valorized, productive population, the development of roads, and the elimination of artificial tariff barriers will permit this new viability of a larger international economic region.

In conclusion, it is necessary to stress the importance of cultural determinants in analyzing man-land relationships. In the twentieth century, the mind of man and of his society is the single most important factor of ecological and geographical change. We can anticipate in the remaining decades of this century an era of over-compensation for former environmental-deterministic modes of thinking. The success of Belo Horizonte and Brasilia, and the highway accomplishments to date should lead to other bolder ventures which should result in the Brazilians putting their imprint on their landscape with even greater confidence. The Brazilian nation in the last half of this century is plugged into the latest technological innovations, wherever they may exist in the world, so it is with some concern that we see in these developments the likelihood that they may force a serious re-evaluation of present policies and practices in anticipation of the imminent problems which lie ahead. Possibly the use of these projective techniques in analyzing landscape changes may help to avoid undesirable outcomes which are foreseen. In conclusion, it is abundantly clear that by the year 2000 A.D. Brazil will definitely still be on the map. We should feel privileged to be able to accompany the developments which lead up to that year.

NOTES ON CONTRIBUTORS

ERIC N. BAKLANOFF, Dean for International Programs and Professor of Economics at the University of Alabama, received his Ph.D. from Ohio State University. From 1950 to 1954 he was associated with the International Division of Chase-Manhattan Bank, including three years with its Puerto Rican branches. He directed Vanderbilt's Graduate Center for Latin American Studies (1962–65) and the Latin American Studies Institute (1965–68) at Louisiana State University, and was a member of the Economics faculty at both universities. His articles have appeared in *Economics Development and Cultural Change, National Tax Journal, Mining Engineering, Journal of Inter-American Studies, Revista Brasileira de Economia,* and other professional reviews. In addition, he edited *New Perspectives of Brazil* (1966) and has contributed to seven other books. A former president of the Southeastern Conference on Latin American Studies (1963–64), Dr. Baklanoff has been the recipient of numerous awards, including a Fulbright grant for research in Chile (1957), NDEA, Ford Foundation, and LSU Foundation grants, and a fellowship (1964–65) from the Center for Advanced Study in the Behavioral Sciences at Palo Alto.

JAMES L. BUSEY, Professor of Political Science at the University of Colorado Cragmor Campus, received his Ph.D. from Ohio State University, and has taught at the University of New Brunswick in Canada and the University of Hawaii. In addition, he held a Fulbright Lectureship in Brazil in 1963. He is the author of *Latin America: Political Institutions and Processes* (1965), *Notes on Costa Rican Democracy* (1962, 1967), and *Latin American Political Guide* (1967). He also contributed to Martin Needler (ed.), *Political Systems of Latin America* (1964) and Bruce Mason (ed.), *The Political-Military Defense of Latin America* (1963). His articles have appeared in diverse professional

157

and scholarly journals, including *Western Political Quarterly, The New Leader, Americas, Social Studies,* and *Historia Mexicana.* His special interests include comparative government and politics (especially Latin America and Canada) and international relations.

MANOEL CARDOZO, Professor and Chairman of the Department of History at the Catholic University of America, received his Ph.D. from Stanford University. He has been twice decorated by Brazil (Rio-Branco Medal, 1945, and Chevalier, National Order of the Southern Cross, 1958) for his distinguished contribution to that nation's historical scholarship. Before joining the faculty of Catholic University he was a Fellow at Instituto de Alta Cultura in Lisbon (1936–38) and has also served since 1940 as curator of the Oliveira Lima Library in Washington, D.C. He has been the recipient of SSRC and American Philosophical Society grants and was appointed Smith-Mundt Visiting Lecturer at the universities in Portugal (1958). A past president of both the American Catholic Historical Association and the Inter-American Council, Dr. Cardozo has contributed to Lawrence F. Hill (ed.), *Brazil* (1947), the *Encyclopaedia Britannica, World Book Encyclopedia,* and *Encyclopedia of Literature.* His articles have appeared in *The Hispanic American Historical Review, The Americas, Hispania, The Catholic Historical Review,* and scholarly journals abroad.

JOHN W. F. DULLES, Professor of Latin American Studies and Brown-Lupton Lecturer at the University of Texas, received his M.B.A. from the Harvard Graduate School of Business and his M.S. from the University of Arizona. He has been associated with United States mining and smelting interests in northern Mexico since 1943. From 1949 to 1959 he held various executive positions with Cia. Minera de Peñoles and Cia. Metalurgica Peñoles. Between 1959 and 1962 he served as vice-president of Cia. de Mineracão Novalimense in Belo Horizonte and Rio de Janeiro. During the summer of 1965 he was director of the Brazil Peace Corps Training Program at the University of Texas. Professor Dulles published *Yesterday in Mexico: A Chronicle of the Revolution, 1919–1936* (1961) and *Vargas of Brazil, A Political Biography* (1967). He has also contributed to scholarly journals, including the *Hispanic-American Historical Review,* the *Southwestern Social Science Journal,* and *Stanford Law Review.* In addition to his professorship, Dulles serves as System Adviser on International Programs at the University of Texas, and has been teaching contemporary Latin American history during alternate semesters at the University of Arizona.

DONALD HUDDLE, Associate Professor of Economics at Rice University, received his Ph.D. from Vanderbilt University where he was also an instructor in Economics. While at Vanderbilt, he was the recipient of an NDEA Fellowship in Economic Development and a grant for dissertation research in Brazil (1962–63). After receiving his degree, he was Visiting Research Economist at Yale (1966–67) and served with the Agency for International Development (AID) as Consultant and Coordinator for Brazilian Research during the summer of 1966. His publications include a monograph, *Fluctuating Multiple Exchange Rates and Economic Development* (1967), and contributions to *Revista Brasileira de Economia, Economic Development and Cultural Change,* and a position paper on U.S. policy in Brazil for the AID.

JOHN V. SAUNDERS, Professor of Sociology at the University of Florida, received his Ph.D. from there and his B.A. and M.A. from Vanderbilt. He taught at Louisiana State University (1959–62), was Fulbright Lecturer at the University of Guayaquil, Ecuador, and served as Area Studies Coordinator for the Peace Corps Brazil Project at the University of Florida. Dr. Saunders is presently consulting editor of the *Journal of Inter-American Studies* and the Language Fellowship Consultant to the U.S. Office of Education. He has also served as contributing editor of the *Handbook of Latin American Studies.* His publications include *Differential Fertility in Brazil* (1958) and *La Población del Ecuador* (1959). From June, 1967, to January, 1969, Dr. Saunders worked as advisor both to the Ford Foundation's population program in Lima, Peru, and to the Center for the Study of Population and Development, an agency of the Peruvian government. His special interests are rural sociology and demography, with a focus on Latin America.

KEMPTON WEBB, Associate Professor of Geography and Associate Director of the Institute of Latin American Studies at Columbia, received his Ph.D. from Syracuse University. He has taught at Indiana University and has served as geographical consultant for numerous agencies and groups, including the U.S. Department of State, Time-Life, Inc., the Odyssey World Atlas, Encyclopaedia Britannica Films and CBS-TV. His extensive field research is reflected in a copious list of publications which includes a monograph, *Geography of Food Supply in Central Minas Gerais* (1959), three books, and contributions to the *Handbook of Latin American Studies, Journal of Inter-American Studies, Annals of the Association of American Geographers,* and other professional journals. Dr. Webb is a member of the Executive Council of the Latin American Studies Association and of the Latin American Research Review Board. He is currently (1968–69) in Portugal as a Fulbright-Hays Fellow doing research on Brazil's historical geography.

INDEX